What
of the
Night?

Selected Plays

★　★　★　★　★

What
of the
Night?
Selected Plays

★ ★ ★ ★ ★ ★ ★ ★ ★

Maria
Irene
Fornes

New York, New York

What of the Night? Selected Plays is published by PAJ Publications, P.O. Box 532, Village Station, New York, NY 10014.

PAJ Publications is distributed to the trade by Consortium Book Sales and Distribution: www.cbsd.com

Publisher of PAJ Publications: Bonnie Marranca

PAJ Publications gratefully acknowledges all those who have contributed valuable advice and research toward the publication of this volume: Morgan Jenness, Micah Bucey, Theresa Smalec, Dawn Williams, Susan Cole, Marc Robinson, Megan Carter, and Susan Ray.

Cover and book design by Susan Quasha

Library of Congress Cataloging-in-Publication Data

Fornes, Maria Irene.
    What of the night? : selected plays / Maria Irene Fornes. – 1st ed.
        p. cm.
    ISBN 978-1-55554-080-7
    1. Title.
    PS3556.07344W48 2008
    812'.54—dc22
                200800351

First Edition, 2008
Printed in the United States of America

Contents

★　★　★　★　★

ABINGDON SQUARE   7

THE SUMMER IN GOSSENSASS   47

WHAT OF THE NIGHT?   97

    Nadine   99
    Springtime   118
    Lust   130
    Hunger   155

ENTER THE NIGHT   171

ABOUT THE AUTHOR   221

Abingdon Square

★ ★ ★ ★ ★ ★ ★ ★ ★ ★ ★

Abingdon Square premiered at The Women's Project & Productions, The American Place Theatre, New York City, October 8, 1987.

CAST

MARION, Madeleine Potter
MICHAEL, John David Cullum
JUSTER, John Seitz
MINNIE, Myra Carter
MARY, Anna Levine
FRANK, Michael Cerveris
THE GLAZIER, Mark Bagnall

The Women's Project & Productions, *Producer*
Julia Miles, *Artistic Director*

Maria Irene Fornes, *Director*

Donald Eastman, *Set Designer*
Anne Militello, *Lighting Designer*
Sam Fleming, *Costume Designer*

CHARACTERS

MARION: From age fifteen to twenty-four.
JUSTER: MARION's husband, from age fifty to fifty-nine.
MICHAEL: JUSTER's son, the same age as MARION.
FRANK: MARION's lover, one year older than MARION.
MARY: MARION's cousin, the same age as MARION.
MINNIE: MARION's great-aunt, from age fifty-eight to sixty-seven.
THE GLAZIER: A very strong, playful man.
THOMAS: MARION's son, eight months old.

ACT ONE: 1908–1912. In a house on Tenth Street, New York City.

ACT TWO: 1915–1917. In the house on Tenth Street, MARY's place, an apartment on Abingdon Square, a beer parlor, and MINNIE's house.

The living room of a house on Tenth Street. To the right is a double door which leans toward the foyer and the main door. On the back wall there are two large French doors. On the right there are double doors that lead to other rooms. Up center, a few feet from the back wall, are a sofa and two armchairs. On each side of the sofa there is a tall stand with a vase. Down left there are a chess table and two side chairs; down right there is a small desk. There is one chair on the upstage side of the desk and another on the right side. During intermission a telephone is placed on the desk.

The attic room or closet. A platform about two feet high on the left side of the stage. On the back there is a small door.

MARY's living room. An embroidered shawl is placed on the sofa.

The living room of an apartment on Abingdon Square. A back wall is placed behind the sofa. On the wall there is a fireplace; above the fireplace there is a large mirror.

The beer parlor. A square plain wood table and two chairs in a pool of red light, center stage.

MINNIE's living room. A chair center stage in a pool of light.

JUSTER's bedroom. A platform about two feet high on the right side of the stage. On the back wall there is a small door. Parallel to the back wall there is a narrow bed.

★ ACT ONE

Scene 1

Tenth Street. August 1908. It is dusk. JUSTER *sits in the garden facing up left. He sings Handel's "Where'er You Walk."* MARION *hides between the two windows and listens.*

JUSTER: *(Singing.)* Where'er you walk,
Cool gales shall fan the glades. *(She moves to the left window and looks at him.)*
Trees, where you sit
Shall crowd into a shade. Trees, where you sit,
Shall crowd into a shade.

MARION: Psst! *(*JUSTER *leans over to see who has called.* MARION *moves her hand towards him.)*

Scene 2

Two weeks later. It is a sunny afternoon. MARION *enters running from the left.* MICHAEL *is chasing her. They run around the room laughing and screaming. He grabs her and takes a piece of chocolate from her hand. He unwraps the chocolate and puts it in his mouth. She chases him. She grabs him and they fall. He covers his mouth. She tries to pull his hand away.*

MARION: Give it to me. *(He swallows the chocolate, lets her remove his hand, and opens his mouth.)*

MICHAEL: It's gone. I swallowed it.

MARION: You're bad! *(She holds him tightly.)* I love you, Mike! I love you. *(He holds her.)*

MICHAEL: Me too! I love you too!

MARION: You are like a brother to me. I love you as a sister loves a brother. But I must love you as a mother. I must be a mother to you. How could a boy like you grow up without a mother? You need a mother.

MICHAEL: You're more to me than any mother could ever be. You're my sister, my daughter, my cousin, my friend. You are my friend! My grandmother!

MARION: You're joking and I'm serious.

MICHAEL: I'm serious. You are to me the best person I'll ever know. The best person I will ever know.

MARION: *(Standing.)* You need a guide, a teacher in life.

MICHAEL: I don't need a guide.

MARION: You need someone who'll tell you what to do.

MICHAEL: I don't. I'm doing fine. I'm a good boy. My mother would say to me, "You're doing fine m'boy. You give me no trouble and you don't need a mother." When I need help I'll go to my best friend, who is you.

MARION: *(As the following speech progresses MARION speaks rapidly as if in an emotional trance.)* You're sweet. You are the sweetest creature on earth. I wish I were sweet like you. I wish I had sweetness in my heart the way you do. Soon I will, officially, be your mother, and I say this in earnest, I hope I can make myself worthy of both you and your father. He brought solace to me when I knew nothing but grief. I experienced joy only when he was with me. His kindness brought me back to life. I am grateful to him and I love him. I would have died had he not come to save me. I love him more than my own life and I owe it to him. And I love you because you are his son, and you have a sweetness the same as his. I hope I can make myself worthy of the love you have both bestowed upon me, and I hope to be worthy of the honor of being asked to be one of this household which is blessed—with a noble and pure spirit. I'm honored to be invited to share this with you, and I hope that I succeed in being as noble of spirit as those who invite me to share it with them. I know I sound very formal, and that my words seem studied. But there is no other way I can express what I feel. In this house light comes through the windows as if it delights in entering. I feel the same. I delight in entering here, and when I'm not here I feel sad. I delight in walking through these rooms, and I'm sad when I leave. I cannot wait for the day when my eyes open from a night's sleep and I find myself inside these walls. Being here I feel as if I'm blessed. If life dealt me a cruel blow when my parents died, now it offers me the kindest reward. I hope I never give either of you cause to regret having invited me to share both your lives. I hope you, as well as he, will always tell me if I have done something wrong—or if you have any reason for disappointment. Would you promise me you will?

MICHAEL: I promise.

Scene 3

A few minutes later. MINNIE and JUSTER are entering from the foyer. MARION stands left.

MINNIE: *(As she goes to sit, to MARION.)* Sit down, dear. *(MINNIE sits right. JUSTER sits left. MARION sits on the sofa.)* I was just talking to Juster about the question of your obligations. The questions you posed to me, and whether you will continue your studies, or what obligations you will have. And we thought you should ask the questions directly to him. The questions you asked me. He doesn't seem to know the answers. Go ahead, dear.

MARION: I wanted to know about my obligations here. I believe that when one marries, one has obligations, and I asked Aunt Minnie what those obligations would be. And she said she was not sure, but that she thought maybe I will be running the house. Is that so? And I told her that I have never run a house, and I don't know if it's something I could learn to do. I told her that I should tell you that I have never run a house. It may be that you don't feel I am suited to do it.

JUSTER: I'm embarrassed to say that I have no idea how to run the house. When I was born my mother ran the house. Then when I was married, my wife Martha ran it. Then when she became ill, Jenny, our housekeeper, took over the running of the house. And when my wife Martha died, Jenny continued running the house until now. I never did.

MARION: And what does running a house consist of?

JUSTER: I don't know, Marion. Minnie, don't you know?

MINNIE: Yes, I do. I run my own house, Juster. But I don't know if you run your house the same way I run mine.

JUSTER: You should talk to Jenny, Marion, and decide what it is you want to do.

MARION: Thank you, I will. Will my cousin Mary continue giving me instructions? I would like to know if that is something I will continue doing—if she will continue tutoring me.

JUSTER: Indeed, Marion, nothing in your life should change unless you want it to.

MARION: Because of all the years I was not able to go to school, I feel I don't yet comprehend a great many things.

Scene 4

Two months later, October 1908. It is dusk. JUSTER *stands center left.* MICHAEL *stands up left.* MARY *stands up right.* MARION *and* MINNIE *embrace center.* MARION *holds a white veil and a missal.* MINNIE *sobs.*

MARION: My dear aunt. I am happy. Believe me, I am happy. I will be very happy. (MINNIE *sobs.* MARION *holds her. A few seconds pass.*) Don't cry, my dear. (MINNIE *sobs.* MARION *holds her. A few seconds pass.*) My dear aunt, don't cry. (MINNIE *goes on sobbing.* MARION *releases her slowly and takes a step away from her;* MARION *lowers her head.* MARY *puts her arm around* MINNIE *and exits with her.* MINNIE *mumbles and cries while she exits.*) Why is she so unhappy?

JUSTER: Weddings make people cry. Marion. (MARION *looks at him.* JUSTER *takes her hand and brings it to his lips. She kisses his cheek.*)

Scene 5

Six months later. April 1909. It is late afternoon. MARION *sits at the desk. She writes in a notebook. There is an open textbook in front of her.* MARY *is standing next to her, leaning over. There is a short exchange of conspiratorial whispering, ear to ear.*

MARY: That's what I heard.

MARION: Who told you?

MARY: My cousin. He knows his family—him and his family. And her and her sister. She also knows him—the man is married. And the wife's sister came to visit. She lives in New Paltz, and her sister, the wife, is also from New Paltz. They're both from New Paltz—his wife and his wife's sister. The sister came to visit, and she stayed for months. The three of them slept together. Together in the same bed. The man and the wife and the wife's sister slept together in the same bed.

MARION: The three of them?

MARY: Yes! The three of them in the same bed.

MARION: Why did they do that?

MARY: To make love!

MARION: How?

MARY: I don't know. I imagine he first makes love to one and then the other. *(Both squeal, terrified and thrilled.)*

MARION: That's perverse!

MARY: That's why I'm telling you.

MARION: It's horrendous!

MARY: I know.

MARION: How did you find out?

MARY: He told me.

MARION: He!

MARY: My cousin.

MARION: How did he know?

MARY: Everyone knows.

MARION: How?

MARY: Noises in the bedroom. The servant heard them.

MARION: It couldn't be true.

MARY: Oh yes, if you see them you would know.

MARION: How?

MARY: The way they look at each other.

MARION: How?

MARY: Obscenely, Marion, and sexually.

MARION: The wife is not jealous?

MARY: No.

MARION: And the sister is not jealous?

MARY: No.

MARION: He looks at them both?

MARY: Yes!

MARION: In the street?

MARY: Yes. He looks at one, then the other—passionately.

MARION: He's shameless.

MARY: The three of them are.

MARION: It's he who does it.

MARY: They too. They also look at him.

MARION: With passion?

MARY: Yes.

MARION: In front of each other?

MARY: They don't mind.

MARION: They don't?

MARY: Apparently not.

MARION: Then the wife's to blame.

MARY: Yes, it's her fault, not his.

MARION: It's his fault, too.

MARY: The sister is pretty. Who can blame him?

MARION: She is?

MARY: Yes. If she lets him, what is he to do?

MARION: He can say no.

MARY: If the wife doesn't mind, why should he?

MARION: Because it's sinful. It's a sin he commits. He will go to hell. God won't forgive him. It's his soul. He can't just say, "They don't mind." He should mind. It is his own soul he has to save. He'll go to hell.

MARY: I know. They'll all go to hell.

MARION: And so will we.

MARY: We?

MARION: For talking about it!

MARY: No, we won't!

MARION: Yes! Because we talked about it, we'll go to hell.

MARY: We didn't do anything!

MARION: Yes, we did!

MARY: What?

MARION: We talked about it and we thought about it.

MARY: Did you?

MARION: Yes.

MARY: What did you think?

MARION: I thought about it. I imagined everything!

MARY: Marion, how could you?

MARION: Didn't you?

MARY: No!

MARION: Oh, God! I've sinned!

MARY: Oh, Marion! Repent.

MARION: I repent! Oh, God! I repent! Oh, God! How could I? Oh, God! *(She falls on her knees. She is out of breath.)* Oh, God! Forgive me! *(She begins to calm down.)*

MARY: *(Kneeling next to her.)* What did you think?

MARION: The three of them in bed.

MARY: What did they do?

MARION: I can't tell you.

MARY: What?

MARION: He makes love to one while the other is there, very close. She looks and she listens. She watches their bodies move. What they say. She's very close.

MARY: How close?

MARION: Touching. She must.

MARY: That's just awful.

MARION: It must be.

MARY: Oh, Marion. And then?

MARION: He kisses her.

MARY: Which one?

MARION: The other one.

MARY: No!

MARION: He holds them both. And knows them both. *(MARY gasps.)*

MARY: Oh, Marion. I too have sinned. Will God forgive us? *(They embrace.)*

Scene 6

One month later. May 1909. It is evening. JUSTER sits up left reading. MICHAEL sits cross-legged on the floor in front of the sofa. He reads a book. MARION sits at the desk. She writes in a diary. The lights are dim except where JUSTER sits.

JUSTER: *(Reading from* My Garden in Autumn and Winter, *by E. A. Bowles)*: "If you wish to see it for yourself, take a pencil and push the pointed end into the open mouth of the flower and downward toward the ovary and the honey, just as a bee would thrust in its tongue. If it is a young flower you have chosen you will see the two anthers bend down as if they knew what they were doing, and touch the pencil about two inches from the point leaving a smudge of golden pollen on it. A day later, the stigma will have lengthened and, if you would, then push your pencil in again. You will find that it now hangs far enough to touch the pencil in the same place where the pollen was laid, while the empty anthers have shriveled. Thus on its first day of opening the anthers rub their pollen on the back of visiting bees; and on the next the stigma hangs down far enough to receive pollen from a younger flower. If you wish to see the mechanism by which the anthers are bent down, cut away the hood until you lay bare the stamens as far as the point where they are joined to the corolla. Here you will notice that they have slender white flying buttresses that keep them in place. Just in front, standing in the tube of the flower, are two white levers growing out from the filaments and blocking the mouth of the tube. Push your pencil in again and see what happens. It strikes against the levers and pushes them down with it. As the buttresses hold the filaments in place, their upper portion is bent over from that point until the anthers touch the pencil."

Scene 7

The attic. Five months later. October 1909. It is morning. MARION stands on her toes with her arms outstretched, looking upward. She wears a white camisole and underskirt. Her whole body shakes with strain. She perspires heavily. On the floor there is a blanket and a large open book. She rapidly recites the following passage from Dante's "Purgatorio" (from the nineteenth-century translation by Henry Francis Cary). MINNIE's words should not interrupt MARION's speech.

MARION: "He girt me in such manner as had pleased
　　　　Him who had instructed; and O strange to tell
　　　　As he selected every humble plant,
　　　　Wherever one was pluck'd another there
　　　　Resembling, straightway in its place arose.
　　　　Canto II: They behold a vessel under
　　　　conduct of an angel.
　　　　Now had the sun to that horizon reach'd,
　　　　That covers with the most exalted point
　　　　Of its meridian circle, Salem's walls;
　　　　And night, that opposite to him her orb
　　　　Rounds, with the stream of Ganges issued forth
　　　　Holding the scales, that from her hands are dropt
　　　　When she reigns highest: so that where I was
　　　　Aurora's white and vermeil-tinctured cheek
　　　　To orange turn'd as she in age increased.
　　　　Meanwhile we linger'd by the water's brink,
　　　　Like men, who, musing on their road, in thought
　　　　Journey, while motionless the body rests.
　　　　When lo! as, near upon the hour of dawn,
　　　　Through the thick vapors Mars with fiery beam
　　　　Glares down in west, over the ocean floor";

MINNIE: *(Offstage.)* Marion …

MARION: "So seem'd, what once again I hope to view,
　　　　A light, so swiftly coming through the sea,
　　　　No winged course might equal its career.
　　　　From which when for a space I had withdrawn
　　　　Mine eyes, to make inquiry of my guide,
　　　　Again I look'd, and saw it grown in size"

MINNIE: *(Offstage.)* Marion …

MARION: "And brightness: then on either side appear'd
　　　　Something, but what I knew not, of bright hue
　　　　And by degrees from underneath it came

Another. My preceptor silent yet
Stood, while the brightness, that we first discerned
Open'd the form of wings: then when he knew"

MINNIE: (Offstage.) Marion, are you there?

MARION: "The pilot, cried aloud, "Down, down; bend low
Thy knees; behold God's angel: fold thy hands:
Now shalt thou see true ministers indeed." (She faints.)

MINNIE: (Offstage.) Marion, are you there? … (A moment passes.) Marion …

MARION: (Coming to.) … Yes. Don't come up … I'll be right down. (MINNIE enters.)

MINNIE: Are you all right?

MARION: … Yes.

Minnie: (Kneeling and holding MARION in her arms.) What are you doing?

MARION: I'm studying.

MINNIE: … You're drenched …

MARION: I know …

MINNIE: Why don't you study where it's cool?

MARION: I have to do it here.

MINNIE: You look so white. (Drying MARION's perspiration.) Look at how you are drenched. Why do you do this?

MARION: I wasn't aware of the heat.

MINNIE: Now you are cold. You are cold as ice. (MARION moves to the left. She leans against the wall and covers herself with the blanket.)

MARION: I feel sometimes that I am drowning in vagueness—that I have no character. I feel I don't know who I am. Mother deemed a person worthless if he didn't know his mind, if he didn't know who he was, and what he wanted, and why he wanted it, and if he didn't say what he wanted and speak clearly and firmly. She always said, "A person must know what he ought to believe, what he ought to desire, what he ought to do." I write letters to her. I know she's dead. But I still write to her. I write to her when I am confused about something. I write and I write, until my thoughts become clear. I want my thoughts to be clear so she'll smile at me. I come to this room to study. I stand on my toes with my arms extended, and I memorize the words till I collapse. I do this to strengthen my mind and my body. I am trying to conquer this vagueness I have inside of me. This lack of character. This numbness. This weakness—I have inside of me.

Scene 8

A day later. Dusk. Juster walks from left to right in the garden. He wears a shirt with the sleeves rolled up. He carries a small tree, whose roots are wrapped in canvas, under his arm.

Scene 9

Five months later. March 1910. It is late afternoon. There is a phonograph on the table. MICHAEL *is placing the needle on a record. It plays a rag.* MARION *and* MICHAEL *dance.*

MICHAEL: That's it. That's it. Good. You're doing well. Ta rah. Pa rah.

MARION: Ta rah. Pa rah. Ta rah. Pa rah. *(They make these sounds through the whole song. The record comes to an end.)* Again ... Let's do it again. *(He starts the record again. They do the dance and sing again.* JUSTER *appears in the vestibule. He hangs his hat on the hatrack. He takes off his coat and hangs it in the closet. He comes into the living room and watches them dance.* MARION *sees* JUSTER *and waves to him. He waves to her.)* Look at me, I'm dancing. Look at this. *(They do a special step.* JUSTER *smiles.)*

MICHAEL: And this. *(He demonstrates another step.)*

JUSTER: That's wonderful.

MICHAEL: Come, learn to do it, Father.

JUSTER: *(Smiling.)* Oh, I don't think I could.

MICHAEL: Yes, yes, you could. I'll teach you. I just taught Marion.

MARION: Oh, yes, it's easy. You just listen to the music, and you immediately start dancing. I learned. You could learn too. I never thought I could learn, and I did. Sing the words, "Tah rah. Pa rah. Tah rah. Pa rah." *(MARION dances toward JUSTER.)*

ALL THREE: *(Singing.)* Tah rah. Pa rah. Tah rah. Pa rah. *(MICHAEL puts JUSTER's arms around MARION in dancing position. The three dance and sing.)*

MICHAEL: Do it! Do it! *(JUSTER takes a couple of steps.)*

JUSTER: Oh, I don't think I can. I never was light on my feet.

MICHAEL: Yes you are, Father. You could do it. You could dance beautifully. You already have the stance.

JUSTER: No, no, I'm sure I can't.

MARION: Do it again. You did it well.

JUSTER: I don't think so. You dance. *(Going to a chair.)* I'll watch you from here. I like to watch you dance. *(JUSTER smiles and claps while they dance.)*

Scene 10

Four months later. July 1910. It is late afternoon. MARION sits at the desk. She is writing in a diary. MICHAEL appears in the doorway to the left. He holds flowers in his hand. He watches her. He tiptoes up behind her and covers her eyes.

MARION: *(Pressing the diary against her chest.)* Oh!

MICHAEL: *(Taking his hand away.)* I didn't mean to scare you. It's only me. I brought you flowers. *(MARION gives a sigh of relief. She closes her diary.)* Don't worry. I didn't read any of it.

MARION: It's a diary. *(MICHAEL sits.)* I was describing an event.

MICHAEL: What event? Is it a secret?

MARION: It's a secret. A meeting.

MICHAEL: What sort of meeting?

MARION: Something imagined. In my mind.

MICHAEL: Diaries are to write things that are true.

MARION: Not this one. This diary is to write things that are not true. Things that are imagined. Each day I write things that are imagined.

MICHAEL: *(Reaching for the diary.)* Could I read it?

MARION: No.

MICHAEL: Why not? If it's things you imagined.

MARION: It would embarrass me.

MICHAEL: Is it romantic?

MARION: Yes. It is the story of a love affair.

MICHAEL: Whose?

MARION: A young man's named F.

MICHAEL: With whom?

MARION: With a young girl.

MICHAEL: What's her name?

MARION: M.

MICHAEL: Who is she?

MARION: Me!

MICHAEL: You!

MARION: Yes! *(He gasps.)*

MICHAEL: You! *(Touching the diary.)* In a romance?

MARION: *(Taking the diary away from him.)* Yes.

MICHAEL: How thrilling!—Do you write each day?

MARION: Yes.

MICHAEL: Since when?

MARION: Since August.

MICHAEL: Do you see him each day?

MARION: No.

MICHAEL: Why not?

MARION: Because I can't.

MICHAEL: Why not?

MARION: I'm married! *(MICHAEL laughs.)*

MICHAEL: Why are you married?

MARION: Because I am.

MICHAEL: If it's imagined, you don't have to be.

MARION: *(Righteous.)* I couldn't do that.

MICHAEL: *(Laughing.)* You're crazy.

MARION: A married woman could not do that. *(She opens her mouth in amazement and they laugh.)*

MICHAEL: Where do you meet?

MARION: In the street. In a parlor.

MICHAEL: Does he come here?

MARION: Here! *(He nods.)* ... No!

MICHAEL: Go on.

MARION: We talk.

MICHAEL: Have you kissed?

MARION: No!

MICHAEL: Will you kiss him?

MARION: I think so. In the future.

MICHAEL: Is he real?

MARION: He is real, as real as someone who exists. I know every part of him. I know his fingernails—every lock of his hair.

MICHAEL: What does F stand for?

MARION: I haven't found out yet. Francis of course. What other name starts with an F?

MICHAEL: Franklin.

MARION: *(Laughing.)* No. His name is not Franklin.

MICHAEL: Of course not. Floyd.

MARION: *(Still laughing.)* No.

MICHAEL: Felix.

MARION: *(Still amused.)* No. Don't say such things.

MICHAEL: I'm sorry.

MARION: Be discreet. You have to know how to enter another person's life.

MICHAEL: I know. I'm sorry. What does he look like? May I ask that?

MARION: He's handsome. He has a delicate face and delicate hands. His eyes are dark and his hair is dark. He looks like a poet. He looks the way poets look. Soulful.

MICHAEL: Where did you first meet him?

MARION: In a shop.

MICHAEL: And you talked?

MARION: Yes.

MICHAEL: Where does he live?

MARION: I don't know yet. I don't know him that well.

MICHAEL: How long have you known him?

MARION: Three months.

MICHAEL: That long?

MARION: Yes.

MICHAEL: How often do you meet?

MARION: Once a week.

MICHAEL: Why not more often?

MARION: I have to be careful.

MICHAEL: Why?

MARION: Because I'm married. *(They laugh.)*

MICHAEL: You're mad. *(She laughs.)*

MARION: I know.

Scene 11

Three months later. October 1910. It is morning. MARION enters right, carrying a hooded cloak. She walks left furtively and looks around. She puts on the cloak, lifting the hood over her head, covering her face. She looks around again and exits right hurriedly.

Scene 12

Three months later. January 1911. It is evening. It is JUSTER's birthday. MARION sits in the chair to the side right; MINNIE and MARY stand by her side. MICHAEL sits on the floor to MARION's right. He holds a ukulele. JUSTER sits in the chair to the left.

MARION: My dear husband, in honor of your birthday, we who are your devoted friends, son, and wife have prepared a small offering—an entertainment. May this, your birthday, be as happy an occasion for you as it is for us. *(MARION extends her hand toward MICHAEL, who starts playing.)*

MARION, MINNIE, MARY, AND MICHAEL: *(Singing "Angry," by Dudley Mecum, Jules Cassard, Henry Brunies, and Merrit Brunies.)*

> "True love never does run smooth
> At least that's what I'm told,
> If that is true then our love surely must be good as gold.
> How we battle every day and when I want a kiss,
> I have to start explaining
> And it sounds about like this:
> 'Dearie, please don't be angry
> 'Cause I was only teasing you.
> I wouldn't even let you think of leavin'
> Don't you know I love you true.
>
> 'Just because I took a look at somebody else
> That's no reason you should put poor me on the shelf.
> Dearie, please don't be angry
> 'Cause I was only teasing you.'"

(They repeat the song. MARION and MARY do a dance they have choreographed.)

MARION: Dear husband, now it's your turn to sing. *(They all gesture toward JUSTER.)*

JUSTER: *(Singing.)* "'Dearie, please don't be angry
> 'Cause I was only teasing you.
> I wouldn't even let you think of leavin'
> Don't you know I love you true.
>
> "Just because I took a look at somebody else
> That's no reason you should put poor me on the shelf.
> Dearie, please don't be angry
> 'Cause I was only teasing you.'"

(MARION kisses Juster on the cheek.)

Scene 13

One month later. February 1911. It is evening. MARION sits in the left chair. MICHAEL lies on the floor. They are both in a somber mood.

MARION: It was he. There was no doubt in my mind. I saw him, and I knew it was he.

MICHAEL: Did he see you?

MARION: No, I hid behind the stacks.

MICHAEL: Then?

MARION: I took a book and buried my head in it. I was afraid. I thought if he saw me, he would know, and I would die. He didn't. I saw him leave. For a moment I was relieved he hadn't seen me, and I stayed behind the stacks. But then I was afraid I'd lose him. I went to the front and I watched him walk away through the glass windows. Then, I followed him ... a while ... but then I lost him because I didn't want to get too near him. I went back there each day. To the bookstore and to the place where I had lost him. A few days later I saw him again, and I followed him. Each time I saw him I followed him. I stood in corners and in doorways until I saw him pass. Then I followed him. I was cautious, but he became aware of me. One day he turned a corner, and I hurried behind him for fear of losing him. He was there, around the corner, waiting for me. I screamed, and he laughed. And I ran. I ran desperately. I saw an open entranceway to a basement, and I ran in. I hid there till it was dark. Not till then did I dare come out. I thought perhaps he was waiting for me. When I saw that he wasn't there, I came home. I haven't been outside since then. I'll never go out again, not even to the corner. I don't want to see him. I don't want him to see me. I'm ashamed of myself. I'm a worthless person. I don't know how I could have done what I did. I have to do penance.

Scene 14

Two months later. April 1911. It is afternoon. MARION stands at the right window looking out. JUSTER is outside. There is a sound of shoveling as JUSTER speaks.

JUSTER: Have you seen the Chinese Holly? It's already budding. It's the first to sprout. It's so eager for spring. Have you noticed how it's grown? It's less than two seasons ago that I planted it, and look how tall it is now. *(Pause.)* Marion—what are you looking at? It's this one I'm talking about. This one here, Marion. *(She walks to the window on the left.)*

MARION: Yes, it is tall.

Scene 15

Ten months later. February 1912. It is evening. MICHAEL and JUSTER play chess at the table to the left. MICHAEL sits to the left. JUSTER stands behind MICHAEL. They both study the board. MARION stands up left. JUSTER turns to look at her.

JUSTER: You look beautiful. You look like a painting. *(She smiles sadly. JUSTER turns to MICHAEL.)* Play, Michael. Make up your mind.

MICHAEL: I don't know what move to make.

JUSTER: Make whatever move seems best to you.

MICHAEL: I get confused. I don't see one move being better than the next.

JUSTER: What do you think, Marion?

MARION: What do I think?

JUSTER: Yes, what should Mike do? Should he scrutinize the board and imagine each move and its consequences, or should he just play and see what happens? I imagine both are good ways of learning. *(As he walks to center.)* One way, I think, is a more Oriental way of learning—through meditation. The other is more Western. Reckless. We are reckless, we Westerners. Orientals meditate until they have arrived at a conclusion. Then they act. We Westerners act. Then we look to see if what we did makes any sense. Which do you think is the best way to act?

MARION: I don't know. I think I'm like an Oriental. I don't think I take chances. I don't take any risks. I don't make any moves at all.

MICHAEL: *(As he moves a piece.)* Check. *(JUSTER looks at the board.)*

MARION: Does that mean you won?

MICHAEL: I don't know. *(He looks at JUSTER. JUSTER looks at him and smiles.)* It's exciting to check though. It's exciting to make a move and be reckless and create an upheaval. And for a moment to think that it's mate. *(To JUSTER.)* Is it?

JUSTER: *(Making a move.)* For now you just lose a bishop.

MARION: Maybe it's best to be like an Oriental.

MICHAEL: I don't know. When you reflect, you have to know what you are reflecting about. When you move without reflecting, *(As he moves a piece, MARION lifts her skirt to see her toes.)* you just move. You just do it. *(She takes six steps looking at her feet.)*

MARION: Six steps and the sky did not fall.

Scene 16

Seven months later. September 1912. It is late afternoon. There are some letters on the chess table. MARION sits in a chair facing the window. FRANK stands in the garden outside the window. MARION's manner of speaking reveals sexual excitement.

MARION: You're trespassing. Where you are standing is private property. It's a private garden, and when strangers come into it we let the dogs out.

FRANK: Let them tear me up. I'll stay here and look at you. *(MARION moves between the two windows. FRANK walks into the living room. She moves to the stage left chair and sits. FRANK follows her and sits at her feet. She starts to go. He grabs her ankle.)*

MARION: Let go.

FRANK: I'm chained to you. I'm your shackle.

MARION: You are?

FRANK: *(Pulling her foot toward him.)* Come.

MARION: *(Pulling back.)* No. Let go.

FRANK: Never. *(She jerks her foot.)* Never. *(She jerks her foot.)* Never. *(She jerks her foot.)* Never. *(She laughs.)*

MARION: What if someone sees you?

FRANK: I'll be arrested.

MARION: Let go of my foot. *(She touches his face. She is scared by her own action and withdraws her hand.)*

FRANK: I know every move you make. I've been watching you. You spy on me, and I spy on you.

MARION: Let go. Someone will see you.

FRANK: There's no one here to see us.

MARION: How do you know?

FRANK: He won't be home for hours.

MARION: Who?

FRANK: Your father. *(MARION is startled by his remark and becomes somber. She walks to the chair next to the desk.)*

MARION: He's not my father.

FRANK: Who is he?

MARION: He's my husband. *(They are silent a moment.)* He is my husband, and I don't want to see you ever again. I am married, and you should not be here. *(Short pause.)* Leave now, please. *(FRANK is motionless for a moment. Then he walks away. JUSTER enters. He opens the closet in the foyer, puts his hat and cane in it, closes the door, and walks into the living room. She is calm and absent, as if something had just died inside her. She sits. JUSTER enters right.)*

JUSTER: Good evening, dear.

MARION: Good evening. *(JUSTER walks left, picks up the mail, and looks through it. He looks at her.)*

JUSTER: Are you all right … ? You look pale.

MARION: Do I look pale? *(He comes closer to her.)*

JUSTER: I think you do.

MARION: I'm fine. *(He kisses her and walks left. He speaks without turning.)*

JUSTER: Is Michael home?

MARION: He's in his room.

JUSTER: Will dinner be at six?

Marion: I believe so. *(JUSTER exits left.)* … I'm sorry … *(FRANK appears again.)*

FRANK: Did you speak to me?

MARION: I'm sorry.

FRANK: You have broken my heart.

MARION: I saw you, and I lost mine. And I also lost my mind. That's why I followed you. I had lost my mind. I thought of nothing but you. Each day I looked for you in the streets. And if not, I dreamt of you. A few days ago I looked outside this window, and I thought I saw you moving among the trees. I thought I was hallucinating. This happened a few times. Were you there? Was that you?

FRANK: Yes.

MARION: What madness. It's my fault. I know it's my fault. I've been married since I was fifteen, and I've never done anything like this. I love my husband and will always be faithful to him. I won't hurt him. He doesn't deserve this. Please leave, or I'll start crying, and they will hear me, and they will come and find me like this. (*After a moment,* FRANK *runs off.* MARION *goes to the couch and sits. She sobs. The lights fade. They come up again. The room is dimly lit.* JUSTER *enters.*)

JUSTER: Have you been here all this time?

MARION: I was looking at the clouds. It seems it's going to rain. (*He looks out.*)

JUSTER: I don't think so. Night is falling. That's why it's getting dark. Dinner is served, dear. Will you come?

MARION: Yes ...

JUSTER: Are you all right?

MARION: ... No ... I'm not feeling very well.

JUSTER: Should you have dinner?

MARION: ... I don't think so ... I'll go up to my room.

JUSTER: May I help you up?

MARION: I'll be up in a moment ... (*He sits next to her.*) What is today's date?

JUSTER: September twentieth.

MARION: Of course. It's the end of summer. The trees are beginning to turn.

JUSTER: Yes. (*She leans on his chest. He puts his arms around her.*)

MARION: Your hands are cold.

JUSTER: There is a change in the air. (*He strokes her hair.*)

★ ACT TWO

Scene 17

Tenth Street. Two years, four months later. January 1915. There is a telephone on the desk. It is early afternoon. The day is overcast. MARION stands by the window to the left. She looks out. She is motionless. An adagio is heard.

Scene 18

Tenth Street. Three months later. April 1915. It is late morning. A vase on the right stand is missing. A GLAZIER is standing on a ladder by the left window. He hammers points on the upper part of the window. He wears belted overalls. MARION enters right. She carries the vase with flowers. She stops to look at him. He continues working. She walks to the right stand. She looks at him again. She is transfixed. He turns to look at her. Their eyes lock. She cannot turn away.

GLAZIER: Could I have a drink of water?

MARION: Yes. *(She does not move. He comes halfway down the ladder and waits. Then he goes close to her, still looking at her. He puts the vase to his mouth and drinks the water through the flowers. She stares. He lets out a laugh. He looks at her.)*

GLAZIER: *(Referring to the water in the vase.)* May I? *(He laughs again. She stares at him. She is possessed. He takes flowers from the vase and puts them in her hair. He then picks her up and carries her upstage. They disappear behind the sofa. She emits a faint sound. The lights fade.)*

Scene 19

Tenth Street. Five months later. September 1915. It is evening. MICHAEL sits left. MARION sits on the sofa. She looks pale and absent. She stares at the floor. JUSTER stands behind the sofa.

JUSTER: I never thought I would have another child. I never thought Marion and I would have a child. I am so much older than she. I am beside myself with joy. Marion is a little worried. She is fearful. You are the first to know. I have suggested she ask Aunt Minnie to come and stay with us. Marion needs a woman's companionship. But she hasn't decided if she'll ask her. Maybe you could persuade her. She has missed you very much. I haven't heard any laughter in this house since you left. Marion has missed you. I hope you will consider going to school in New York this year. Marion is desolate, Michael. Would you consider returning home? *(JUSTER looks at MARION. He then looks at MICHAEL helplessly. MICHAEL looks at MARION. He is pained.)*

MICHAEL: I will think about it, Father.

Scene 20

Tenth Street. One year later. September 1916. It is late morning. Center stage, there is a rocking horse. On the horse, there is a teddy bear. MARION enters from left. She carries THOMAS, eight months old. She takes the teddy bear. FRANK appears outside the window.

FRANK: Hello.

MARION: … Frank …

FRANK: My name is not Frank.

MARION: It isn't? *(He shakes his head.)* What is your name?

FRANK: Jonathan.

MARION: Jonathan?

FRANK: Yes.

MARION: Your name is not Frank? *(She laughs.)* That's not possible.

FRANK: My name is Jonathan. I was named after my father. *(She laughs.)*

MARION: I'm so happy.

FRANK: Why?

MARION: I'm so glad to see you. *(She sighs.)* Where have you been?

FRANK: I was away.

MARION: Where were you?

FRANK: In Michigan.

MARION: What were you doing in Michigan?

FRANK: Working with my uncle. Have you thought of me?

MARION: Oh, yes.

FRANK: What have you thought?

MARION: That I love you. *(Pause.)*

FRANK: What a pleasant surprise. *(Starting to step in.)* May I come in?

MARION: *(Laughing.)* No.

FRANK: Come outside then.

MARION: Not now.

FRANK: When?

MARION: Tomorrow.

FRANK: At what time?

MARION: At one.

FRANK: Where?

MARION: In the square.

FRANK: Abingdon?

MARION: Yes.

FRANK: *(Moving his hand toward her.)* See you then.

MARION: *(Her fingers touching his.)* See you.

Scene 21

Tenth Street. Five months later. February 1917. It is evening. MARION sits to the left of the chess table. MICHAEL sits down right.

MARION: He often speaks of closing the house and moving south, where the weather is temperate. He likes using that word: temperate. It's quite clear why he does. He means moral balance. Evenness of character. He means that he knows what I do when I leave the house. That he knows about Frank and me. He's saying that he'll seek moderation at any cost. That he's ready to divorce me and put an end to our family life. I'm ready for it. I'm ready to face him with it. He's just making it easier for me. *(MICHAEL looks down.)* What's the matter?

MICHAEL: When I'm with him, I care about nothing but him. *(They look at each other for a moment.)* I love him. He's my father and I love him. And

I don't want to see him suffer. When I'm with you, I forget that he's my father and I take your side. He's my father, and I love him and I respect him. And I feel terrible that I've been disloyal to him. And I feel worse to see that he's still gentle and kind to both you and me. I'm sorry, because I love you too, and I know that you, too, need me. But I can't bear being divided, and I have to choose him. I'm leaving, Marion. I can't remain here any longer knowing what I know and feeling as I do about it. It's too painful, and I'm demeaned by my betrayal of him. There are times when I want to tell him the whole truth. And if I don't, it's because I love you, too, and I feel there's no wrong in what you're doing. I really don't. I think you're right in what you're doing. You're young, and you're in love, and it's a person's right to love. I think so. Frank is handsome, and I think he is honest. I mean, I think he loves you. He's not very strong, but he's young. No one is strong when he is young. I'm not. Only I'm still playing with soldiers, and he has entered into the grownup world. If I were in his place, it would terrify me to be the lover of a married woman. Goodbye, my sister. I must leave. I am constantly forced to act in a cowardly manner. I cannot be loyal to both, and I cannot choose one over the other, and I feel a coward when I look at you, and I feel a coward when I look at him. I am tearing out my heart and leaving it here, as half of it is yours, and the other half is his. I hope I won't hurt you by leaving—beyond missing me, which I know you will. I mean beyond that. I mean that I hope my leaving has no consequences beyond our missing each other. Take care. *(He starts to go, then turns.)* What if you're discovered? Will he get a job, take on such responsibility? Will he marry you?

MARION: ... I don't know. I haven't thought about that ...

JUSTER: *(Offstage right, in a disconnected manner.)* Are you leaving? *(A short pause.)* Are you staying for dinner?

MICHAEL: I have some studying to do.

JUSTER: *(Offstage.)* Stay. We should be eating soon. You could leave after dinner. We should have dinner soon. *(He enters and walks to center with a glazed look. He stops, still facing left, and looks at the floor as he speaks.)* How are you, my dear?

Marion: ... Good evening ...

JUSTER: You both look somber. I hope nothing's wrong.

MARION: ... No, nothing's wrong.

JUSTER: *(Walking left as he speaks.)* I've had a bad day myself. Sit down, Michael. I'll be back in a moment. *(The volume of his voice does not change as he leaves the room.)* I'll be back in a moment. *(There is the sound of water running as he washes his hands.)* It was difficult at work today. Everyone seems to be constantly shirking responsibility. That seems to be the main problem in the world today. It's not possible to get things done properly, either in the house or at work. Will the person whose duty it is to prepare dinner be here on time to prepare it? Will that person be at the market early enough to ensure that the ingredients he gets are fresh and not wilted and sour? *(He enters drying his hands with a hand towel.)* Will my office staff appear at work properly dressed and properly shaven? It seems as if each day the lesson has to be taught again. The same lesson. Each day we have to restore mankind to a civilized state. Each night the savage takes over. We're entering the war. I'm sure we are. In no time we will be in the middle of a war. Yes, you wash your face! Yes, you comb your hair! Yes, you wear clothes that are not soiled! Why can't people understand that if something is worth doing, it's worth doing right! *(He sits down and puts the towel on his lap with meticulous care. He takes off one of his shoes.)* I take care of my feet. My socks are in a good state of repair. When they wear out, I pass them on to someone who needs them. *(Taking off his other shoe.)* Others mend their socks. I don't. I don't mind wearing mended clothes. My underwear is mended. So are my shirts. But not my socks. *(With both feet on the floor.)* I have always wanted to give my feet the maximum of comfort. It is they that support the whole body, yet they are fragile. Feet are small and fragile for the load they carry. I wear stockings that fit so they won't fold and create discomfort to my feet. If I treat my feet with respect, my brain functions with respect. It functions with more clarity, and so does my stomach. I digest better. In the morning at the office, I look at my mail. Then I call my assistant. I discuss some matters with him. Then I call my secretary. She comes in with her stenographer's pad and sits down on the chair to my right. I collect my thoughts for a few moments. *(Standing.)* Then I stand on my feet, walk to the window at my left, and from there, standing on my feet with my stomach properly digesting my breakfast and my brain as clear as the morning dew, I dictate my letters.

MARION: I will go see if dinner is ready. *(She exits left.)*

JUSTER: What is wrong with Marion? She's not herself.

MICHAEL: Nothing. Nothing I know of.

JUSTER: What is wrong with you? What is the matter with you?

MICHAEL: Nothing, Father.

JUSTER: Have you thought it over?

MICHAEL: What?

JUSTER: Are you coming home?

MICHAEL: Not yet. *(JUSTER sits.)*

JUSTER: Fine. You do as you must, Michael. *(There is a pause.)* It is hard to know whom to trust, whom to show your heart to. *(He picks up his shoes and puts them on his lap.)*

MARION: *(Offstage.)* Dinner is ready.

JUSTER: Come, Michael. *(MICHAEL walks up to JUSTER and waits for him. JUSTER is still sitting.)* Let's have dinner.

Scene 22

Tenth Street. Two weeks later. March 1917. It is late afternoon. MARION and FRANK are embracing in the space behind the sofa. She speaks with urgency.

MARION: I have been warned that this is a dream. That tomorrow you won't love me. I've been told I must prepare myself. That when you leave me, my life will end. That my pain will be eternal. Hold me. Hold me in your arms. *(He does.)* Something terrible is happening. Something terrible happens each day. You're not touched by it—but I am impure. I lie and lie each day, every minute, every hour. I am rotten and deceitful. Except to you, each time I speak, I tell a lie. I am deceitful. I am impure. How I wish I could spend my days with you, only with you, and with no one else. And to speak only the truth ... only the truth ... only the truth. *(There is a pause.)* Frank, wouldn't you like it if we spent all our time together, day and night? If we traveled together? If we walked on the street together, holding hands? If we spent our evenings together sleeping in each other's arms? How would you like that? *(There is a silence.)* Frank ...

FRANK: We have to be careful.

Scene 23

Tenth Street. Two weeks later. Evening. MARION sits at the desk and prepares to write. JUSTER enters from the garden. He looks at her for a while. Then he walks quietly to her side. He caresses her hair, then tightens his fist around it. She lets out a whimper. He holds onto her hair, then releases it. She is frightened and motionless. He stares at her for a while longer. He then takes a paper from his pocket and puts it on the desk. She looks at it, lowers her eyes, and remains motionless.

JUSTER: *(Threateningly.)* Do you know what this is? *(She looks away.)* What is it? *(Pause.)* Tell me!

MARION: *(In a deadened tone.)* A receipt.

JUSTER: For what? *(Pause.)* For what?

MARION: For an apartment.

JUSTER: For what purpose? *(Pause.)* For what purpose? *(She starts to rise. He puts his hands on her shoulders, forces her to sit, and continues to put pressure on her. In a quiet, controlled voice.)* What have you done? *(Pause.)* What have you done? *(They look at each other. She is unflinching. He puts pressure on her shoulders until she falls to the floor. He takes a chair and raises it over his head to hit her. She screams. He stops himself. He puts the chair down and exits left. She rises slowly, goes to the left window, and looks. FRANK enters from the right. She turns to him. She is confused. They walk to each other. She starts to gesture towards the garden nervously. He takes her hand. She starts to pull it away. JUSTER enters the garden. She looks towards the garden. JUSTER goes to the window and looks in. JUSTER looks at them. The lights begin to dim.)*

Scene 24

Tenth Street. A few hours later. JUSTER sits at the desk. He opens the drawers, takes out letters, deeds, notebooks, address books, checkbooks, photographs, documents, and ledgers, and arranges them on top of the desk rapidly. JUSTER's briefcase is on the floor, next to the desk. MARION enters. She stands left. JUSTER ignores MARION and takes out a few more papers.

JUSTER: What are your plans?

MARION: In regard to what?

JUSTER: In regard to your life!

MARION: I've not made any plans.

JUSTER: Well, do. I'd like to know what you intend to do. How soon can you decide? I want to know what you plan to do as soon as possible. *(He places the briefcase on his lap and puts the papers in the briefcase as he speaks.)* I expect you to leave as soon as possible. I expect you to move your things, what you can, today. A few things. What you need for immediate use. The rest I'll have sent to the place you choose. If you have a place of your own, you should move there. *(She starts to speak. He continues.)* Thomas will stay with me. *(She starts to go.)* Don't bother to look for him. Don't think you're taking him with you. You'll waste your time looking for him. He's not in the house. I have taken him to a place where you won't find him, and no one but I knows where that is. So don't bother to look for him. *(MARION reenters.)* I am leaving now. I'll return later tonight. When

I return, I expect you'll be gone. Jennie will help you pack, and she will take you and whatever things you want to that place or any other place you wish. If you don't leave, you'll never see Thomas. You're an adulterous wife, and I'll sue you for divorce. A court will grant me sole custody of the child. Do you have anything to say? *(There is a moment's silence.)*

MARION: I will not leave unless I take Thomas with me.

JUSTER: If you're still here when I return, you'll never see him again. *(MICHAEL enters right. JUSTER speaks to him.)* Marion is leaving tonight, and she'll never enter this house again. She's not wanted here. She has debased this house. She will not be forgiven, and her name will never be mentioned here again. And if you think of her ever again, you'll never enter this house.

MICHAEL: Father, may I intercede?

JUSTER: In regard to what!

MICHAEL: Father—

JUSTER: *(Interrupting.)* No. I will not hear what you have to say. I don't want your advice. Marion will leave. You may escort her wherever it is she is going if you wish.

Scene 25

MARY's place. Two months later. May 1917. It is evening. MARY sits on the sofa. JUSTER sits left. He wears a hat and coat and holds his briefcase on his lap.

JUSTER: I never saw myself as deserving of her love. She was precociously beautiful, modest. She was thoughtful and respectful. There was no vanity in her. When her mother died, I don't believe she cried once, but her spirit left her. She seemed absent. This was the way she grieved. She was obedient. She did what was asked of her, but she had lost her sense of judgment and her desire to choose one thing over the other. She accepted what others chose for her. She sat for hours staring into space. I took her for walks. I took her to the park. We took boat rides. Our meetings became more frequent. We were natural companions. I loved her company, and I found myself always thinking of her. She was sad and still when I wasn't there. When she saw me, she smiled and came to life. Her aunt told me this, too. That she only smiled when she saw me. I foolishly believed that this meant she loved me. I proposed marriage, and she accepted. Her aunt, too, thought it natural when I asked for her hand in marriage. She gave us her blessings. There was no exuberant joy in our wedding, but there was the most profound tenderness. I was very happy, and I thought

Marion was also. There were times when she was taciturn, but I thought she was still grieving for her mother. She was a child, and she needed a mother more than a husband. But a husband is all she had. I could not be a mother to her. Seven years later Marion had a child. I was overwhelmed with joy, but Marion was not. She became more taciturn than ever. *(There is a pause.)* I began to feel she hated me. And she does hate me, and she has made me hate her. You see her. I know you see her. I know you go to that apartment frequently. I've seen you go in. *(Pause.)* Tell me, Mary, what is she like with him? *(Pause.)* War has been declared, and I'm afraid that Michael will be drafted. He, too, will be taken away from me.

Scene 26

Abingdon Square. Two weeks later. June 1917. It is evening. MARION stands left. MARY sits right. They drink vermouth and smoke.

MARION: I am in a state of despair! Thanks to Frank. How could I not be? *(Turning to MARY.)* Why did you do that? *(To MARY.)* Have you ever lived with someone who speaks one way and acts another? Someone for whom words mean nothing? Or if they mean anything, they mean something different from what they mean to you? My life is a puzzle. I don't know where I stand. I am constantly asking: What do you mean? What is it you mean? What does that mean to you? Why did you say that? Why did you do that? Have you?

MARY: Me? *(MARION sits left.)*

MARION: When I sinned against life because I was dead, I was not punished. Now that life has come unto me, I am destroyed, and I destroy everything around me. May God save me. I have always trusted in His goodness and His divine understanding. May God have mercy on me. I have never denied Him.

Scene 27

A beer parlor. Two weeks later. Evening. A square table. JUSTER sits left. MICHAEL sits right. There is a glass of beer in front of each. JUSTER speaks obsessively.

JUSTER: I have tried. I offered her some money. She didn't accept it. I knew she wouldn't. She stared at me and said nothing. We were in a public place. She stared, and I waited for her to answer. After a while, I knew she had no intention of answering. I said to her, "Do you have anything to say?" She still said nothing, but I felt the hatred in her eyes. I said, "I suppose you are not accepting my offer?" She said nothing. I said, "For

God's sake, say whether you don't accept it or do, and if you don't, let's get on to something else." Her hatred is such, it burns. Paper would burn if it were held up to her glance. When I reached the door, I saw her back reflected in the glass. She was so still, there was no life in her. She was still like a dead person. I regretted having offered her the money. I had no reason to think she would accept it. What do they live on? *(Short pause.)* Have you seen her?

MICHAEL: No.

JUSTER: She's gone berserk. She is wild like a madwoman. She's insane. You haven't seen her?

MICHAEL: No.

JUSTER: You haven't been in touch at all? Letters?

MICHAEL: No.

Juster: Last week I followed her to a dance parlor. *(MICHAEL looks at him.)* Yes, Michael. You have not been here, and you don't realize what's going on. Marion's behavior is irrational. She's not sane. I followed her, and she went into a dance parlor. It was still light outside, and yet people were already dancing. I followed her in, and I took a table by the window. A man wearing a soldier's uniform greeted her. They started dancing. And moved to a dark corner. She knew I was there looking at her, and that's why she did what she did. They kissed and caressed lewdly. I've never seen such behavior in public. Never did I think I would see someone ... I so cherished behave like that. She knew I was there. She knew I could see them, and yet she did what she did. *(He takes a drink.)* One day last week, she came to my office. I was standing by the window. I did not notice her at first. Then I heard her say, "Does this happen every afternoon?" I turned to her. She had been standing at the door. And I said, "Does what happen every afternoon?" She said, "Do you stand at the window every afternoon?" I said, "Yes." And she said, "What do you look at?" I said, "I look out. I don't look at anything in particular. I look out because that's how I concentrate on what I have to do." "And what is it you have to do?" "Right now I'm in the middle of dictating my letters." Then she stood behind my secretary and leaned over to look at her writing pad. Then she said, "What is that? A secret code?" Shorthand! Then she came to where I was. She said to me, "That is a love letter." She then looked out the window and said, "Do you use binoculars?" I told her that I could see quite well without binoculars, and she said, "From where you are, can you see the house on Abingdon Square? Can you see it? Can you see it?" She thought I was spying on her. She's mad. She's capable of anything. *(He looks absently as he takes a revolver from his pocket and puts it on the table.)* I carry this with me at all times. I don't know if I will shoot her, or if I will shoot myself. I know one of us will die soon.

MICHAEL: ... Father ... I must try to stop you. (JUSTER *puts the revolver in his pocket. He takes a purse out of his pocket, takes money out, and puts it on the table. He stands and starts to walk away. He stops.*)

JUSTER: Would you take care of the bill, Michael?

MICHAEL: ... Yes ... (JUSTER *starts to exit.*) Father ... I've enlisted. (JUSTER *stops, looks at* MICHAEL *for a moment, turns slowly away, and exits.*)

Scene 28

Abingdon Square. Two weeks later. July 1917. MARION *stands up left.* MARY *sits right.*

MARY: Who? Juster?

MARION: Yes, Juster. I hate him. I will shoot him. I imagine I shoot him, and I feel a great satisfaction. A satisfaction equal to flushing a toilet, seeing the water flush out and vanish forever. I am crude. I know I'm crude. I know I'm uncivilized. I know I am a part of a civilized race, but I am uncivilized. Thomas is not his!

MARY: Marion!

MARION: He's not.

MARY: Is he Frank's?

MARION: No.

MARY: Whose is he?

MARION: (*She lets out a loud laugh.*) A stranger's. A stranger. Just someone. Someone who came into the house one day and never again. I never saw him again. Just a man. A stranger. No one. I have a bad destiny, Mary. I have an evil destiny. It constantly thwarts me. Nothing comes to me at the right time or in the right way.

Scene 29

MINNIE's *living room. One week later. It is evening.* MINNIE *sits on a chair, center stage.* MARION *is on her knees facing* MINNIE.

MARION: I need my child. I need my child, Minnie. I need that child in my arms, and I don't see a way I could ever have him again. He has been irrevocably taken from me. There is nothing I could do that would bring him back to me. I have begged him to let me see him. I have gone on my knees, I have offered myself to him. I have offered my life to him. He won't listen to me. He won't forgive me. I'm at his mercy. I wish for his death. I stalk the house. I stand on the corner, and I watch the house. I imagine the child inside playing in his room. When spring comes, I may be able to see him in the garden. I know he's not there, but that's how I can feel him near me. Stalking the house.

MINNIE: Why won't he let you see him?

MARION: He's gone mad! He's insane, Minnie.

MINNIE: Juster?

MARION: Yes! He's insane! He wants to destroy me. But I'll destroy him first.

MINNIE: Marion, I don't understand you. I forget things. I'm too old. I don't remember what you're talking about. It's no longer in my mind. *(Touching the side of her head.)* The flesh is sore and swollen. This part of it is stretched and redder than the rest, as if it's hotter. As if it had a fever. As if it had hair. It throbs.

Scene 30

Tenth Street. A few days later. It is late morning. JUSTER sits at the desk. He speaks to MICHAEL on the phone. After a few moments, MARION appears outside the left window. She is spying on JUSTER.

JUSTER: She follows me. She's insane. She's jealous, Michael. She is jealous of me. Her jealousy is irrational. As irrational as everything else she does. *(MARION makes a move and makes a noise. JUSTER turns toward her. To MARION.)* What are you doing?

MARION: Who is here with you?

JUSTER: I'm alone. I'm talking on the telephone. *(She hears a sound and turns to the left.)*

MARION: What was that? Someone's in the back. *(She exits left. He speaks to MICHAEL.)*

JUSTER: She is outside. Doing who knows what in the garden. She just looked through the window and demanded to know who is here with me. There is no one here with me. Not even Jenny is here. I have sent her away. I prefer to be alone. *(MARION enters right.)*

MARION: Who are you with?

JUSTER: I am with no one.

MARION: Who are you talking to?

JUSTER: I'm talking on the telephone. *(She takes the receiver from him, listens for a moment, shakes the receiver, blows on the mouthpiece, and hangs up. She walks around the room.)*

MARION: I love this house. I had forgotten how I love this house. *(Pause.)* I have been ill. I have had fevers. *(Pause.)* I'll tell you a riddle. See if you can solve it:

> If a person owns an object, where is it? It's under his arm.
> If a person loves an object, where is it? It's in his arms.
> If a mother's baby is not in her arms, where is it?

(Pause.) Where is it? Where is Thomas? Where have you taken him? Is there someone in your life? Someone influencing you? How can you do this? How can you put me through this? What do you gain?

Scene 31

Abingdon Square. Two weeks later. August 1917. It is evening. The stage is dark. There is the sound of gunshot. The lights come up. JUSTER stands downstage facing up. He wears an overcoat and a bowler hat. His right arm hangs, holding a revolver. MARION is up center. She faces him. Her arms are halfway raised and her mouth and eyes are open in a state of shock. MARY enters running from left. MARION turns to look at MARY. Both JUSTER and MARION go through the motions he describes.

JUSTER: I came in. I said nothing. I took the gun out and aimed at her. She stared at me. Her courage is true. She stared at death without flinching. My eye fell on the mirror behind her. I saw my reflection in it. I am much older than she. Much older. I looked very old, and she looked very young. I felt ashamed to love her so. I thought, "Let her young lover kill her, if she must die." I turned the gun to my head. She moved toward me calmly. She put her hand on mine and brought it down away from my head. She said, "Please." I was moved by her kindness. I turned to look at her. And again I was filled with rage. My finger pulled the trigger. *(He shoots again. MARION screams, runs upstage, and returns to her position at the start of the scene.)* That was the blast you heard. The gun was aiming at the floor. Everyone here is perfectly all right. *(JUSTER begins to choke. It is a stroke.*

He turns front slowly. He starts to walk backwards gasping for air. He falls unconscious on the sofa. His eyes are wide open.)

Scene 32

Tenth Street. A month later. September 1917. It is dusk. FRANK stands behind the couch to the left. MARION sits right of the couch. She is serene and composed.

FRANK: And if he doesn't come to, will you spend the rest of your life taking care of him?

MARION: When I reach out to touch him, I don't know if I'm reaching outside of me, or into me. If he doesn't come out of the coma ... ? I feed him. I bathe him. I change him. I wait for the day when I can speak to him ... speak to him at least once.

FRANK: I wanted to ask you if there is anything I can do.

MARION: ... No ... Thank you, Frank. *(FRANK sits on the right side of the couch.)*

FRANK: I may be leaving once again, Marion.

MARION: Oh ... ?

FRANK: Yes, I may be moving on.

MARION: I know, Frank. I know you must go. *(They sit silently for a while.)*

Scene 33

JUSTER's bedroom. A day later. It is evening. JUSTER lies in his bed unconscious. He is in a coma. He is unshaven. MARION stands on the upstage side of the bed. JUSTER begins to come to. His speech is impaired.

JUSTER: ... It looks much nicer here than in the parlor ...

MARION: What does?

JUSTER: ... It feels bad.

MARION: What feels bad?

JUSTER: ... It is happier here ...

MARION: What?

JUSTER: It's happier. Don't you know it?

MARION: What? *(His eyes open.)*

JUSTER: Who's here?

MARION: It's me.

JUSTER: Who?

MARION: Marion.

JUSTER: Marion?

MARION: Yes.

JUSTER: Why are you here?

MARION: Because you're ill.

JUSTER: What's wrong with me?

MARION: You had a stroke.

JUSTER: What have you done to me!

MARION: Nothing.

JUSTER: Yes, you have.

MARION: What have I done?

JUSTER: You've done harm to me.

MARION: No. *(He looks at her suspiciously.)*

JUSTER: What have you done to me? Get out!

MARION: I've nursed you. I've fed you.

JUSTER: What have you fed me? *(She is silent.)* Poison!

MARION: No.

JUSTER: I hate you! You're repulsive to me! *(Pause.)* You've touched me!

MARION: Yes.

JUSTER: Do you enjoy seeing me like this! *(Pause.)* Where's Michael? *(Pause.)* Has he been here?

MARION: I sent for him.

JUSTER: I want to see him.

MARION: He's trying to get here.

JUSTER: Why can't he come?

MARION: They won't give him leave.

JUSTER: *(Starting to get out of bed.)* I want to get up. *(During the following lines, he tries to get up, and she tries to stop him.)* I want to be downstairs when he calls.

MARION: He won't call till later.

JUSTER: I'll call him.

MARION: He can't be reached. *(He collapses.)*

JUSTER: Am I dying?

MARION ... I don't know. *(He tries to get up.)*

JUSTER: I don't want you here. *(She takes a step back.)* Get out! Get out! *(She starts to leave, then stops.)* Get out!

MARION: ... May I come back later? *(He does not answer.)* I understand. *(She exits. He lifts himself to a sitting position, stands, and stumbles to the living room.)*

JUSTER: ... Marion ... Marion! *(He starts to fall.)* ... Marion ... *(He crawls.)* Marion ... Marion ... *(MARION runs in. She holds JUSTER in her arms.)* I love you.

MARION: ... I love you too. *(She sobs. MICHAEL enters, walks to them, and stands behind them. He wears an army uniform. There is a shaft of light behind him. As MARION speaks, JUSTER's hand begins to rise.)* Michael ... ! Michael ... ! He mustn't die! He mustn't die! Don't die ... ! Don't die ... ! *(His hand touches her face.)* ... He'll be all right. He'll be all right.

The Summer in Gossensass

★ ★ ★ ★ ★ ★ ★ ★ ★ ★ ★ ★ ★ ★ ★ ★ ★

The Summer In Gossensass premiered at The Women's Project & Productions, Judith Anderson Theatre, New York City, March 31, 1998.

CAST

ELIZABETH ROBINS, Molly Powell
VERNON ROBINS, Daniel Blinkoff
MARION LEA, Clea Rivera
LADY BELL, Valda Setterfield
DAVID, Joseph Goodrich

Made possible by a grant from TCG/Pew Charitable Trusts.

The Women's Project & Productions, *Producer*
Julia Miles, *Artistic Director*

Maria Irene Fornes, *Director*

Donald Eastman, *Set Designer*
Philip Widmer, *Lighting Designer*
Gabriel Berry, *Costume Designer*

CHARACTERS

ELIZABETH ROBINS: Actress, playwright, essayist.
MARION LEA: Actress.
VERNON: ELIZABETH's brother. A medical student.
DAVID: An actor.
LADY BELL: Essayist, reporter, and lover of the arts.

A large studio-living room, usually associated with the work/living quarters of painters. Up right is the main entrance, up left is a door that leads to the kitchen; up center is a curtain that leads to ELIZABETH's sleeping quarters. Center stage is a round table. To the right of the table there is a chaise longue. Against the left wall there is a bookcase-desk. On this desk is a kerosene lamp. In various areas of the living room there are some stuffed chairs, straight-back chairs, and small tables. On the table and on the floor around the table there are several books.

Scene 1

London, February 1891.

ELIZABETH and MARION are sitting at the table. They each hold a book. There are other books on the table and on the floor. LADY BELL sits in an armchair a few feet upstage. She reads a newspaper. There are candles or kerosene lamps to read by. There is an air of ease and tranquility.

ELIZABETH: Ibsen said that anyone who wished to understand him must understand Norway.

MARION: Did he say that?

ELIZABETH: Yes.—He said that the severe cold and lonely life have an influence on Norwegians.

MARION: Hmm.

ELIZABETH: He said in Norway winters are long, and Norwegians spend long days waiting for spring. He said Norwegians brood and are apt to despair.—He said Norwegians are not capable of folly.

MARION: He *is* serious.

ELIZABETH: Yes.

MARION: He broods.

Elizabeth: Yes.

Marion: He says in Norway things don't change easily.

ELIZABETH: Hmm …

MARION: Yet, in the 1870s, the Bohemian movement caused quite a stir.

ELIZABETH: Oh?

MARION: Listen. *(Reading from one of the books.)* "In most of Europe, where freedom of expression and people's rights to dispose of their own lives were a given, the Bohemian movement was not considered a threat. It was an artistic expression. However, in Norway it caused quite a stir. It was believed that such philosophy would destroy the moral and legal structure of the Nation. The inner circle of the movement was composed of musicians, painters, writers, and critics. Their battleground was their studios, the coffee houses, and their dingy bed-sitting rooms. They abhorred all authority, regarded all leadership an abomination, and considered free love a natural right. Hans Jaeger was their leader. His enemies considered him the arch-priest of the devil. In the heat of battle, the Boheme adopted slogans which were scandalous. They encouraged their followers to seduce the daughters of the bourgeoisie and to drive their sons to suicide."

ELIZABETH: Heavens.

MARION: Listen to this.—These are their nine commandments: —"Thou shalt create thy own life.—Thou shalt sever all family ties.—One cannot treat one's parents badly enough."

ELIZABETH: *(Reaching for the book.)* Let me see. "Thou shalt never owe thy neighbor less than five Kroner." You should owe him more than five Kroner.

MARION: Oh. *(Reading.)* "Thou shalt hate and despise all peasants such as Bjornson."

ELIZABETH: Who is Bjornson?

MARION: A peasant. "Thou shalt never wear celluloid cuffs."

ELIZABETH: Celluloid?

MARION: Yes. "Never fail to create a scandal in the Christiania Theatre."

Elizabeth: Hmm.

MARION: Too conservative.—"Thou shalt never feel regret."

ELIZABETH: Why not regret?

MARION: An aimless exercise in self-deprecation.

ELIZABETH: I see.

MARION: And … last is, "Thou shalt take thine own life."

ELIZABETH: Goodness!

MARION: Yes.

ELIZABETH: How shocking.

MARION: That is their aim.

ELIZABETH: To shock.

MARION: How odd.

ELIZABETH: Yes. Was Ibsen in Norway then? Was he a bohemian? No.—Was he their friend? What did he think?

MARION: Was he scared of them?

ELIZABETH: No.—Yes. *(Short pause.)* Of course. He would have been. Think of him.—Not scared. But not very much at ease.—Yes.—He would have been. Scared. Think of him. Restrained. Formal.—Observant.—Like a wild animal. He's shy, bewildered. Always thoughtful, seeking, always, intensely. Always. Not fearful. Courageous. He would not be scared of bohemians. Scared of others perhaps but not of them. They were artists as he.—He delves into unimaginable depths … Oh, the things he knows. Oh.—Oh yes. *(Short pause.)*

MARION: What about his new play, Elizabeth, have you heard? Is his main character, Hedda, a bohemian? Is she?

ELIZABETH: … I don't think so.

MARION: She's very wild.

ELIZABETH: Very wild, and yet very conventional.

MARION: What makes you think that?

ELIZABETH: She's wild, and yet submissive. A conformist—has a taste for wildness and a taste for conformity. I have known women like that.—All men are like that.—But women are not. Not so often. Women are either conformists, or they are nonconformists. Being wild may be her downfall. Hedda's downfall. But I believe first was her downfall, and then her wildness. I know that can happen.

MARION: The wildness comes from despair?

ELIZABETH: Sometimes, yes. Sometimes it comes because something has changed inside.

MARION: What has changed?

ELIZABETH: A light has gone out inside.

MARION: What causes the light to go out? … I don't know. What is that light?

ELIZABETH: It's something that makes us feel joy, feel compassion, feel for others.

MARION: Do you think she fell from grace?

ELIZABETH: Yes.

MARION: Yet you care for her.

ELIZABETH: Yes.

MARION: As if she were a real person.

ELIZABETH: Yes. I can't help caring for her. As if she were real. She's bad, and yet I care for her.

MARION: She doesn't feel pain?

ELIZABETH: One wishes she would.

MARION: Does she feel compassion?

ELIZABETH: No.

MARION: Does she have any redeeming qualities?

ELIZABETH: Yes.

MARION: What?

ELIZABETH: She doesn't lie. I don't think she lies.

MARION: She's true.

ELIZABETH: She doesn't mind a negative opinion of her.—She has a sense of humor.

MARION: That is a redeeming quality.

ELIZABETH: Yes.

MARION: Will they save her ... these qualities?

ELIZABETH: I don't know.

MARION: What else?

ELIZABETH: She's beautiful and she's intelligent.

MARION: And besides lacking compassion, does she possess any other unfavorable qualities?

ELIZABETH: In plays, unlike real life, characters may not always have a past, but they will always have a destiny. The destiny of this character is to turn on herself and to consume herself. Like an uroboros.

MARION: What is an uroboros?

ELIZABETH: It's a reptile that swallows its own tail until it has consumed itself. She moves in concentric circles. Things outside those circles she doesn't see. The things she doesn't see don't burden her.—She's impervious to them.

MARION: One would not think these are attractive qualities.

ELIZABETH: *(Laughs.)* But they are.—And she is also sociable. She finds amusing things in people. Even people who are without interest. And yet she lacks compassion. But she may find something amusing about people who are compassionate. She doesn't enjoy their company. That is what I think she lacks. Not pity, I don't mean pity. She lacks pity also, but what I'm talking about is something else. She is not moved to experience the experience of others. Not moved to experience what another person is experiencing. I think that is what is lacking in her. That is what we feel when we're near her. She's not mean. She doesn't take pleasure in the pain of others. She may if it's interesting. She is playful, mischievous. She has faults. But the worst thing is that she doesn't understand. She may suffer from intermittent amnesia of things that are unpleasant. Would she be hurt if someone doesn't like her hat? No. She couldn't care less if someone doesn't like her hat, so she finds it curious and amusing if someone else finds it hurtful. There are things others see that she is blind to. She doesn't believe they exist. In her house she is a queen. She doesn't like to venture out-of-doors.

MARION: What are you thinking?

LADY BELL: What are you thinking, dear?

ELIZABETH: She's a prisoner.

LADY BELL: What makes you think that?

ELIZABETH: She is cloistered.

LADY BELL: You think someone keeps her imprisoned?

Elizabeth: It may be her own doing. Is she hiding something? I would like to know ... Is she always in her house? *(VERNON enters.)* Vernon ...

VERNON: What?

ELIZABETH: What does it mean when a person doesn't leave the house?

VERNON: *(From the threshold.)* A person who doesn't leave the house is a person who likes to stay home.

ELIZABETH: No, silly, a person who is *afraid* to leave the house.

VERNON: That's an agoraphobic.

ELIZABETH: What does that mean?

VERNON: An agoraphobic is a person who does not dare go out in the open, a person who fears open spaces.

LADY BELL: Oh, Vernon, that is so exciting! She fears open spaces.

MARION: Oh, she's an agoraphobic uroboros.

LADY BELL: An agoraphobic uroboros. That makes so much sense.

MARION: We've found the key to Hedda Gabler's character.

LADY BELL: *Bravi, bravi.*

VERNON: She's an agoraphobic uroboros.

LADY BELL: Well, aren't you playful.

ELIZABETH: If she doesn't play, she becomes ill.

LADY BELL: What games does she like to play?

ELIZABETH: Cat-and-mouse.

LADY BELL: With whom?

MARION: With whomever is available.

LADY BELL: Who's the cat? And who's the mouse?

MARION: She's always the cat.

ELIZABETH: That's interesting.

LADY BELL: Not to some … Some prefer to be the mouse.

MARION: And if she can't play, what illness overcomes her?

ELIZABETH: Boredom.

LADY BELL: Ah.

MARION: Can doctors cure boredom?

LADY BELL: No, they can't.

ELIZABETH: Is her illness contagious?

MARION: The illness is not.

ELIZABETH: What is contagious?

MARION: She is.

ELIZABETH: What are the symptoms?

MARION: One succumbs to her charm.

ELIZABETH: Everyone?

MARION: She's irresistible.

ELIZABETH: Is she bright?

MARION: More so than those around her.

LADY BELL: Who is around her?

ELIZABETH: We'll see when we get the play.

LADY BELL: You're being secretive.

ELIZABETH: I haven't figured it out yet, but I think she's magnificent.

MARION: And you'll play her exquisitely.

ELIZABETH: No, Marion, you should play her.

MARION: No, Elizabeth, it's you who should play her.

ELIZABETH: You should.

MARION: No, you should.

ELIZABETH: It's you who should.

MARION: You must.

ELIZABETH: Why, Marion?

MARION: Look at your eyes.

ELIZABETH: Why my eyes?

MARION: Lady Bell, don't you think?

LADY BELL: *(Looking up from her book.)* What, Marion?

MARION: Don't you think Elizabeth should play Hedda Gabler? She has the eyes.

LADY BELL: What sort of eyes does Hedda Gabler have?

MARION: Look at Lady Bell, Elizabeth.

LADY BELL: What sort of eyes does Elizabeth have? Yes. Those are Hedda Gabler's eyes.

MARION: See?

LADY BELL: And are we expecting to see Mr. Ibsen's play?

MARION: Well, it's going to be published in Munich.

LADY BELL: If we don't get it soon, I'm sure you'll write your own verses.

MARION: Oh, if one only could. However, I have written to a friend in Munich asking him for details.

LADY BELL: I see.

ELIZABETH: Has he seen the play?

MARION: If he was in Munich, I'm sure he did see it. I hope he was there. If he was, he must have seen it. Of course he did. How could he have not? He would have seen it if he was there.

LADY BELL: Well, let's hope …

ELIZABETH: Yes.

LADY BELL: My, my, what have we here?

ELIZABETH: What is it?

LADY BELL: There is a notice here on the very subject of which we speak. This critic says, referring to Hedda, *(Reading.)* "A monster in female form to whom no parallel can be found in real life." Does he not like the play? Or is it the lady he doesn't like? Or is he saying that a well-mannered lady in our civilized would should not have inclinations such as this Hedda; therefore, we should not enjoy the play? Or, does he mean that he wouldn't want to be married to the lady? I think that's what he means. Well, I don't suppose Mr. Ibsen is proposing that this critic should marry this lady. Would this critic, when reviewing *Medea,* say that he doesn't like the lady and he would not like to marry her? *(She looks at another review for a moment.)* There is more. This one says she's "a horrid miscarriage of the imagination." Is it that they don't like the play? If they don't like the play, why don't they just say so? Where do we find these critics?

MARION: Lady Bell, do you think Hedda Gabler resembles a woman Ibsen loves?

LADY BELL: *(Laughs.)* A real woman?

MARION: Well, yes.

LADY BELL: That Hedda is not a woman invented by his creative imagination, but that he knew such a woman and took her spirit, her essence, for this play?

MARION: Yes.

LADY BELL: What an idea. That is so interesting, Marion. Isn't it, Vernon? That she is not a character whose every characteristic is imagined by the author, invented by the author, but a character created by the author from the existence, inspired by the existence of a real person. That is, a creation based on an existing person. Not a biographical study. Of course a biographical study is an obvious study of a person. With a name and a history. A date of birth.—And one could also create a character in a play from that. But we're thinking of a creation imagined, inspired by the existence of a living person. Not completely accurate, faithful to the details of the person's life, but with invented details. Details based on the essence of the person. Isn't that fascinating.—So an author could be conversing with you. Becoming interested in you, in the way you see things. In how your life has evolved; in the existence of you, a real person, who then inspired in the author the desire to create a personage in his play, a personage who embodies your essence. Not an invented personage created for the purpose of the play, but a play created to embody the essence of a real person. That is fascinating, Elizabeth, Marion, Vernon, that from the essence of a real person, an artist can create a fictitious character.

VERNON: Psychologists have psychoanalyzed fictional characters. Fictional characters who never existed, characters created by the imagination of the author. In spite of their being unreal, psychologists have psychoanalyzed them and have come up with astonishing findings. Take this character of Hedda, for example. One could take this character and psychoanalyze it as if it were a person. For example, one could say that in a situation when others feel compassion, she may feel boredom. When others may feel insecure or distressed, she begins to get distracted and bored. That she doesn't understand worrying or being shy, or being insecure, or being hurt. She has never felt those things. She can be kind if you don't bore her. If you bore her, you disappear. She may just make a face of slight displeasure, and you cease to exist. You see what I mean. You can understand things like that about a fictional character. As a student of medicine, I have come to the conclusion that this woman possesses an abnormal psychology.

ELIZABETH: Vernon, I think you're right. I take it she's not normal.

LADY BELL: Elizabeth, I don't know that there is a real woman who has inspired this play. I wonder about that. I wonder if Ibsen's talent didn't simply create Hedda without that external inspiration. He is very talented. And quite capable of inventing her. But if there is such a woman, did he write the play to offend her? To keep her at bay? Was this how he expressed devotion to her? Do you know?

ELIZABETH: No, Lady Bell, I don't know anything beyond what we've heard here. I feel Hedda is quite an extraordinary person. She may be the invention of a great master, or she may be a real person who inspired the master. In either case, I would like very much to play her. Unless, Marion, you are interested in playing her.

MARION: Well, Elizabeth. *(Pause.)*

VERNON: *(Looks at his watch.)* Oops! I have to go now. I have a class. *(VERNON starts to go.)*

ELIZABETH: Bye, Vernon.

VERNON: Bye, Elizabeth.

MARION: Goodbye.

VERNON: Goodbye, Marion.

LADY BELL: Goodbye, Vernon.

VERNON: Goodbye, Lady Bell.

Scene 2

Later that evening.

There is the dim light of dawn from the back window. MARION sleeps on the settee. VERNON enters. He looks around. He goes to the table, sees the books on the floor, picks them up, takes them to the desk, goes to where MARION sleeps, and looks at her. MARION stirs and continues sleeping. He returns to the table, takes a book out of his pocket, takes a note out of the book, looks at it a moment, and puts it on the table. He then sits down, opens the book, and reads awhile. As the lights begin to fade, he puts the book down, slides himself to the floor, rests his head on the floor, and goes to sleep.

Scene 3

Dawn. The following day. MARION sleeps on the settee. VERNON is asleep under the table. The entrance door opens. DAVID puts his head in. He looks at a paper in his hand, looks at the room, looks at the door for a sign. Looks around the room again. Takes a step out and closes the door. A moment later, ELIZABETH enters from the left. She walks to the table and stumbles on VERNON.

VERNON: Ouch!

ELIZABETH: Oh!

VERNON: … What …

ELIZABETH: *(Affectionately.)* What are you doing here?

VERNON moans.

ELIZABETH: How long have you been here?

VERNON moans.

ELIZABETH: Vernon, why are you on the floor?

VERNON: … I fell asleep …

ELIZABETH: Wouldn't you like to lie on a bed?

VERNON: I'm all right.

ELIZABETH: When did you come in?

VERNON: A while ago … *(He lifts his head up as if to rise and returns to a sleeping position on the floor.)* Did you see the note?

ELIZABETH takes the note from the table.

ELIZABETH: Who is this?

VERNON: A friend of Sven's.

ELIZABETH: What about him?

VERNON: He has a copy of Ibsen's new play.

ELIZABETH: ... Of the new play?

VERNON: Yes.

ELIZABETH: Here?

VERNON: It's being published.

ELIZABETH: Here.

VERNON: Yes, here.

ELIZABETH: In English.

VERNON: In Norwegian.

ELIZABETH: In Norwegian?

VERNON: Yes.

ELIZABETH: In London.

VERNON: Yes.

ELIZABETH: In Norwegian.

VERNON: Because of a new law.

ELIZABETH: What law?

VERNON: A law that allows the publisher of the original work in the original language to have exclusive world rights not only for publication, but also for stage productions.

ELIZABETH: Oh.

VERNON: They only printed twelve copies and got all these rights. It's a new law.

ELIZABETH: Printing just twelve copies gives them that right ... an exclusive world right ... for publication ... and production?

VERNON: Yes.

ELIZABETH *looks at the note.*

Elizabeth: ... And this fellow has a copy ... How is that possible? And who is the publisher?

VERNON: Edmund Gosse.

ELIZABETH: Did you see it?

VERNON: No, but this fellow who has it says he'll let you look at it.

ELIZABETH: Has it been translated?

VERNON: No.

ELIZABETH: Will Archer be the translator?

VERNON: No.

ELIZABETH: Who will be the translator?

VERNON: Edmund Gosse.

ELIZABETH: Does Edmund Gosse know Norwegian?

VERNON: No.

ELIZABETH *gasps.*

ELIZABETH: Does Archer know this?

VERNON: I don't know. *(Indicating the paper on the table.)* That's the fellow's address.

ELIZABETH: What fellow?

VERNON: The fellow who has the play.

She looks at the paper closely.

ELIZABETH: You think I could see it?

VERNON: He said you could. Sven also mentioned someone named David whose interest in theatre has caused him to collect documents and memorabilia of theatre artists for whom he has special admiration. He has papers on Ibsen and papers from Ibsen's very hand which he may be willing to share with us. Some of them, Sven says, are related to the play that interests us.

MARION begins to stir. He goes to MARION.

VERNON: *(Whispering.)* Good morning, Marion. How nice to see you.

MARION: *(Opening her eyes.)* … Good morning … How are you, Vernon?

He sits by her.

VERNON: I'm all right.

ELIZABETH: Tell her, Vernon.

MARION: … What?

VERNON: A friend of Sven's has a copy of Ibsen's new play in Norwegian, and he'll let you see it. He also knows someone who may let us see some letters and notes that relate to the play we want to do.

MARION: Oh, how wonderful to wake up with such news.

VERNON: I'm so glad. *(He turns to ELIZABETH and speaks cautiously.)* … Elizabeth, there's something else I have to tell you.

ELIZABETH: What?

VERNON: *(Speaks with caution.)* … Sven says the English rights for production have also been assigned.

ELIZABETH: *(Gasping.)* They have!

MARION: What?

VERNON: Yes.

ELIZABETH: *(Restlessly.)* To whom?

VERNON: To McArthy.

ELIZABETH and MARION pace restlessly.

ELIZABETH and MARION: McArthy … ?! McArthy … ?!

VERNON: It's even worse.

ELIZABETH: Worse!

MARION: What!

VERNON: Worse.

ELIZABETH: What is worse!

VERNON: There is something worse.

ELIZABETH: How can there be something worse?

MARION: What can be worse!

VERNON: I think there is.

ELIZABETH: What is?

VERNON: I believe the role of the main character ... Hedda ... has already been cast.

ELIZABETH and MARION hyperventilate.

ELIZABETH:	MARION:
Oh! Oh! Oh! Oh!	Oh! Oh! Oh! Oh!

VERNON: I believe there is an actress who is doing it.

ELIZABETH and MARION gasp.

VERNON: Yes.

ELIZABETH and MARION mumble and pace.

VERNON: Yes, an actress is doing it. Please, calm down.

ELIZABETH: Oh my God!

MARION growls.

VERNON: It has in fact been cast.

MARION: ... No ... !

VERNON: Calm down!

ELIZABETH: I'm calm!—Who have they cast?

VERNON: Marion, you know how things are in the theatre.

MARION and ELIZABETH pace and moan.

MARION:	ELIZABETH:
How are things in the theatre?	What else! What else!

VERNON: You know that sometimes the wrong person is cast in a role.

ELIZABETH and MARION growl.

VERNON: *(Raising his voice.)* What is the matter with you two?

ELIZABETH: Nothing!

VERNON: You, Marion. What is the matter with you?

MARION: Who—has—been—cast!

VERNON: Sit down!

ELIZABETH: Who, Vernon? Who—has—been—cast? Who!

MARION: *(Grabbing* VERNON *by the collar.)* Who! Who! Who! Who! Who! Who! Who! Who!

VERNON: Lily Langtry! Lily Langtry! Is—playing—Hedda! … Hedda!—Hedda Gabler!—Lily Langtry! Is playing Hedda! Ga-bler!

ELIZABETH *and* MARION *gasp, are short of breath, pace back and forth, and speak and mumble words of disapproval.*

VERNON: Calm down!

ELIZABETH: Lily Langtry! Lily Langtry!

MARION: How did this happen! How is this possible!

VERNON: Calm down! Calm down!

ELIZABETH: … Lily Langtry?! *(She gasps for air. She convulses.)*

MARION: Not possible!

ELIZABETH: Playing Hedda?! Playing Hedda?!

MARION: Playing Hedda?!

VERNON: Lily Langtry! Lily Langtry!

MARION: It's not possible! It's not possible! Who told you! Who told you, Vernon?!

VERNON: Sven! Sven told me!

ELIZABETH: It's not possible! Can she act?!

MARION: Lily Langtry!

ELIZABETH: Has she ever acted?!

Marion: Lily Langtry!

VERNON: Calm down! Calm down!

ELIZABETH: Bring Sven here! Bring him here! How can he say such a thing?!

VERNON: What have I done! What have I done! Who is this Hedda! Who is this Hedda! Who is this Hedda! Who is this Hedda that makes you act this way! Who is this Hedda that makes you act like two crazy women! Calm down! Calm down!

MARION: *(Shaking VERNON.)* Where! Where is this happening!

VERNON: Here! Here! In London! Right here! Lily Langtry is playing Hedda! So there!

ELIZABETH and MARION, exhausted and dumbfounded, sit. They now speak softly.

MARION: Is that *the* Lily Langtry?

VERNON: Yes …

There is a moment's silence.

VERNON: She has taken up acting.

ELIZABETH: She has?

VERNON: Yes.

There is a moment's silence.

VERNON: To please the Prince of Wales.

ELIZABETH and MARION whimper.

VERNON: The Prince and she are … in a liaison.

ELIZABETH and MARION whimper.

VERNON: Yes. He has taken a liking to her.—And they wish for her to perform in serious dramatic roles.

They whimper. The lights fade.

Scene 4

Two days later.

Light comes up slowly on ELIZABETH, *who sits at the table examining the Nor-wegian copy of Ibsen's play. On the table, there are a Norwegian dictionary, a notebook, and a pencil.*

ELIZABETH: *(Reading from the book and looking up each word in the diction-ary.)* Du ... *(Writing.)* you. *(Looking it up.)* Vel ... *(Writing.)* well. *(Look-ing it up.)* Taenke ... *(Writing.)* thank you. *(She looks at what she's written.)* "*Det kan du vel taenke. General Gablers datter.*"—"It can you well, thank you." Hmm ... What could that possibly mean? "It can you well." "It'd do you well or good." "It could do you good." Or, "It would be good for you, General Gabler's daughter."—Or, "It will behave well with you." Or, "It will behave well for your sake." *(She takes the book in her hands and holds it against her chest.)* I have the play ... It's in my hands. But I can't read it ...

There is the sound of steps and a knock on the door.

ELIZABETH: Marion ... ?

ELIZABETH exits.

MARION: *(Offstage.)* It's me.

ELIZABETH: ... Marion ... did you go?

MARION: Yes.

ELIZABETH: Did you see a rehearsal?

They enter. MARION *wears a hat and coat and carries a purse.*

MARION: No.

ELIZABETH: ... Oh.

MARION: There was no rehearsal.

ELIZABETH: ... Oh.

MARION: The place was dark, but I opened the door and went in. There was no one there.

ELIZABETH: You went in?

MARION: I went in and sat down. I thought I'd wait. I thought they'd soon be coming in to rehearse. After a while, I noticed a note on the table.—It said, "Tonight's rehearsal cancelled." But I stayed, and I got used to the darkness and started looking around. Then I saw a door and opened it. It led to a larger room, and I went in. The first room was an office. The second one was much larger.—It must be where they rehearse. There was almost no furniture in it. I walked to a window and looked out. It was dark and quiet out. Then I saw a comfortable chair and sat down. I stared at the place, and I imagined the play going on. *(She closes her eyes.)* I imagined people talking to each other. I couldn't hear the words, but I could hear the sound of their voices, and I could see how they moved, and I could sense how they felt about each other. Then you came in. You were playing Hedda Gabler. Someone stood and went to speak to you. You were courteous and elegant. Someone else came to join you. You went to a chair and sat down. One of the others also sat, and the other stood at your side. You talked to each other. Then you stood up, said a few words and started walking away. Someone walked towards you and caught up with you. You exchanged a few words, and then you turned and looked at some of the people in the room. Then you walked up again and left the room ...

ELIZABETH: ... I did all that ... ?

MARION: Yes. I imagined it. After a while, I went to the first room again, and I noticed some pages in the waste basket. *(She reaches inside her coat.)* I took them. I took them, and I put them inside my coat. And I left. I thought they were pages from the play. And I took them. They were being thrown out.

ELIZABETH: In English?

MARION: Yes.

ELIZABETH: From the play.

MARION: They must be.

ELIZABETH: You didn't read them?

MARION: No.

ELIZABETH: You didn't ...

MARION: *(Hands some pages to ELIZABETH.)* I wanted to read them, but I waited to read them with you. There are some pencil notes on them. Some acting notes, I think, ... or some changes.

ELIZABETH: Thank you, Marion.

MARION: You have no idea how thrilled I am.

ELIZABETH: *(Holding the pages against her chest.)* I do. I'm thrilled, too.

MARION: I walked here. I wanted to run. But I walked as fast as I could. I didn't want to attract attention to myself.

ELIZABETH: Would you like some tea?

MARION: Yes, please.

ELIZABETH puts the pages down, but her eyes fall on the words, and she starts reading.

MARION: When I saw there was no one there, I thought, if I see the translation, I'll stay all night and copy it. And if someone comes in, I'll hide till they leave. And then I'll continue copying it. But I found this. In the wastebasket. It's in English! It's part of the translation. On the way here, I was tempted to stop and read it under a lamppost. But I thought someone may be following me, so I came here directly.

ELIZABETH: My goodness, Marion.

MARION: No one followed me, though. If they did, they will soon be knocking at the door ... *(Becoming alarmed.)* If they do, don't open it. *(Pause.)* When you've done something wrong, you think you're being followed. But you still do it, because you have to do it. It's not rational. It's that you're scared. You're terrified. You think you'll be caught.

ELIZABETH: Poor Marion. And to think I was just sitting here in a warm room.

MARION: Yes. I felt like a thief.

ELIZABETH: *(Touching her nose affectionately.)* You are a thief ... I'll get the tea.

As ELIZABETH begins to turn, her eyes fall on the pages on the table. Her head leans toward them slowly. She turns slowly towards MARION and starts to read.

ELIZABETH *(As HEDDA.):* "Love, how funny you are."

MARION: "It is not love then?"

ELIZABETH: "Hush!"

VERNON enters. He wears a coat. They look at him.

VERNON: What?

ELIZABETH: *(Reading.)* "Tesman enters with a small tray."

VERNON: What?

ELIZABETH: Read with us?

VERNON: What?

ELIZABETH: *(Turning her pages to VERNON.) Guess* what we've got.

VERNON: What?

ELIZABETH: *Look at this.*

VERNON: *Oh my God.*

ELIZABETH: Read Tesman.

VERNON: Who is Tesman?

ELIZABETH: We don't know.

VERNON: Don't I need to know who I'm playing? Is this an old man? Is this a banker, an artist, a baker? Is he heavy? thin?

ELIZABETH: We'll find out, Vernon. Please read.

VERNON: *(As TESMAN.)* "Here you are! Doesn't this look good?" *(Reading as he gestures.)* "He puts the tray down." *(As VERNON.)* The tray looks good.

ELIZABETH: *(As HEDDA.)* "Berte could have brought it."

VERNON: *(Doing it.)* "Filling the glasses." *(As TESMAN.)* "I enjoy doing it, Hedda."

MARION: Who is Tesman?

VERNON: He's a servant.

ELIZABETH: He's not a servant.

VERNON: Why not?

ELIZABETH: Would he call her Hedda if he were?

VERNON: No.

ELIZABETH: He may be a relative.

VERNON: And bring a tray? That's not right.

ELIZABETH: Maybe he's being courteous.

VERNON: That's possible.

ELIZABETH: *(As HEDDA.)* "You poured out two glasses. Mr. Lovborg said he won't have any." He's not a servant, but he's acting like a servant.

VERNON: *(As TESMAN.)* "But Mrs. Elvsted will soon be here, won't she?"

ELIZABETH: *(As HEDDA.)* "Oh, of course,—Mrs. Elvsted."

MARION: Uh-oh. She doesn't like Mrs. Elvsted.

VERNON: *(Studying the script.)* It's true, I noticed that, too. You can tell when a person doesn't like another just from the lines. Isn't that amazing.

ELIZABETH looks at him.

VERNON: *(Reads.)* "Had you forgotten?"

ELIZABETH: *(As HEDDA.)* "We were so absorbed in these photographs." *(She turns her script toward VERNON.)* "What is the name of this little village?"

VERNON: *(As TESMAN.)* "That's Gossensass. Just below the Brenner Pass. Fancy—if we could have had you with us, Ejlert! Eh?" *(Pause.)* Who's Ejlert?

ELIZABETH: We'll see.

VERNON: *(Turning as if to leave. Reading.)* "He exits." *(As himself to ELIZA-BETH.)* Do I exit?

ELIZABETH: No, you stay.

MARION and ELIZABETH sit on the bench. Their movements are a stylized version of polite manners. VERNON sits at a distance.

ELIZABETH: *(As HEDDA.)* "There! We've killed two birds with one stone."

MARION: *(As THEA.)* "What do you mean?"

ELIZABETH: *(As HEDDA.)* "I wanted to get rid of him."

MARION: *(As THEA.)* " ... So he'd write the letter?"

ELIZABETH: *(As HEDDA.)* "So I'd be able to speak to you."

MARION: *(As THEA.)* "About the same thing?"

ELIZABETH: *(As HEDDA.)* "Yes."

MARION: *(As THEA.)* "But there isn't anything else to say, Mrs. Tesman. Nothing at all."

ELIZABETH: *(As HEDDA.)* "Oh yes there is. There's a lot more—I can see that. Sit here—and we'll have a cozy, confidential chat." *(She takes MARION's hand and brings her to sit next to her.)* Vernon, would you take some notes? If we do the play, it'd be good to have them.

MARION: *(As THEA.)* "But my dear Mrs. Tesman—I should be leaving now."

ELIZABETH: *(As HEDDA.)* "Oh, there's no hurry.—Tell me a little about your life—at home. It will all come out anyway!"

MARION: *(As THEA.)* "That's the last thing I care to speak about."

ELIZABETH: *(As HEDDA.)* "Not to me, dear? Weren't we friends at school?"

MARION: *(As THEA.)* "You were one class ahead of me. I used to be afraid of you."

ELIZABETH: *(As HEDDA.)* "Afraid of me?"

MARION: *(As THEA.)* "Yes, very. You pulled my hair in the stairs."

ELIZABETH: *(As HEDDA.)*: "Did I?"

MARION: *(As THEA.)* "Yes, and once you said you would burn the hair off my head."

ELIZABETH: *(As HEDDA.)* "It was only in fun."

MARION: *(As THEA.)* "Yes, but I was very silly in those days.—And since then, anyway, we have drifted so far apart. Our circles have been very different."

ELIZABETH: *(As HEDDA.)* "Well, let's see if we can drift closer together again. At school we used to confide in each other, and we called each other by our first names."

MARION: *(As THEA.)* "Oh no, you're mistaken."

ELIZABETH: *(As HEDDA.)* "'Not at all! I remember very well. So now we are going to renew our friendship.' *(She gets closer to MRS. ELVSTED.)* 'There now!' *(She kisses her cheek.)* 'You must talk to me like a friend and call me Hedda.'" *(MRS. ELVSTED presses and pats HEDDA's hands.)*

MARION: *(As THEA.)* "Oh, you're so kind! I'm not used to this kindness."

ELIZABETH: *(As HEDDA.)* "There, there! And I'm going to treat you like a friend, as I did before, and call you my dear Thora."

MARION: *(As THEA.)* "Thea."

ELIZABETH: *(As HEDDA.)* "Of course. I meant Thea. You're not accustomed to goodness and kindness, Thea ..."

MARION: *(As THEA.)* "No."

Short pause.

ELIZABETH: I don't think it should be done this way. I don't think it is that well-mannered. I think they say what they mean. I think in this world, in this world of Ibsen's Norway, they are more direct even in polite society, even if there are complicated things happening to them. Hedda, however, is very curious, and yet she doesn't ask direct questions. She asks questions, but she is evasive. And Thea is afraid of something, but she doesn't say what she is afraid of. I don't think they are reserved. I think something important is happening. Not just to Thea. Obviously something very important is happening to her, and she doesn't want to talk about it to this woman, Hedda, who professes to be her friend. But something important is also happening to Hedda. Something important is happening to both. I wish we had a few more pages. Can't you get a few more pages?

MARION: I'll try.—I think it's possible that Thea has taken something from Hedda. And that she thinks that Hedda suspects her. And that her questioning, Hedda's questioning, will soon lead to this thing she has taken. I think that's why she's nervous. She seems to be afraid that Hedda will, sooner or later, bring it up.

ELIZABETH: ... Taken what?

MARION: Maybe money.—Or a piece of jewelry. Don't you think she's acting guilty about something?

ELIZABETH: Who, Thea? Yes! There's something to that. And Hedda is trying to catch her, isn't she? She wants Thea to confide in her. She says, "At school you used to confide in me."

MARION: Yes. I'm going to try to get in there again tomorrow. See what I can find. These pages are good, but they're not enough. Not enough at all.

ELIZABETH: Would you?—Would you like me to go with you?

MARION: No, it's better if I go alone. Less noticeable.

ELIZABETH: However, we could still do more work on these.

MARION: Yes.

ELIZABETH: Shall we?

MARION: Yes.

They repeat the scene. The approach is now more complex, as there is an effort from both to reach the other, as well as to understand her own position.

ELIZABETH: More direct.

MARION: Less reserved.

ELIZABETH: Less guarded. *(As HEDDA.)* "There! We've killed two birds with one stone."

MARION: *(As THEA.)* "What do you mean?"

ELIZABETH: *(As HEDDA.)* "I wanted to get rid of him."

MARION: *(As THEA.)* " … So he'd write the letter?"

ELIZABETH: *(As HEDDA)* "So I'd be able to speak to you."

MARION: *(As THEA.)* "About the same thing?"

ELIZABETH: *(As HEDDA)* "Yes."

MARION: *(As THEA.)* "But there isn't anything else to say, Mrs. Tesman. Nothing at all."

ELIZABETH: *(As HEDDA)* "Oh yes there is. There's a lot more—I can see that. Sit here—and we'll have a cozy, confidential chat." *(She takes MARION's hand and brings her to sit next to her.)*

MARION: *(As THEA.)* "But my dear Mrs. Tesman—I should be leaving now."

ELIZABETH: *(As HEDDA)* "Oh, there's no hurry.—Now, tell me a little about your life at home. For it will all come out anyway!"

MARION: *(As THEA.)* "That's the last thing I care to speak about."

ELIZABETH: *(As HEDDA)* "Not to me, dear? Weren't we friends at school?"

MARION: *(As THEA.)* "You were one class ahead of me. Oh, I used to be afraid of you."

ELIZABETH: *(As HEDDA)* "Afraid of me?"

MARION: *(As THEA.)* "Yes, very. You pulled my hair on the stairs."

ELIZABETH: *(As HEDDA)* "Did I?"

MARION: *(As THEA.)* "Yes, and once you said you would burn the hair off my head."

ELIZABETH: *(As HEDDA)* "It was only in fun."

MARION: *(As THEA.)* "Yes, but I was very silly in those days.—And since then, anyway, we have drifted so far apart. Our circles have been very different."

ELIZABETH: *(As HEDDA)* "Well, let's see if we can drift closer together again. At school we used to confide in each other, and we called each other by our first names."

MARION: *(As THEA.)* "Oh no, you're mistaken."

ELIZABETH: *(As HEDDA)* "'Not at all! I remember very well. So now we are going to renew our friendship.' *(She gets closer to MRS. ELVSTED.)* 'There now!' *(She kisses her cheek.)* 'You must talk to me like a friend and call me Hedda.' *(HEDDA presses and pats MRS. ELVSTED's hands.)*"

MARION: *(As THEA.)* "Oh, you're so kind! I'm not used to this kindness."

VERNON: Elizabeth. What is it that I should note down?

ELIZABETH: Just what we do. Where we go. Write down what we do.

VERNON: You mean, as when you hold her hand?

ELIZABETH: Yes.

VERNON: And when you stood up on the line, "Well, let's see if we drift closer together again"?

ELIZABETH: Yes, that's right.

VERNON: And when you put your hands on her shoulders and say, "So now we're going to renew our friendship"?

ELIZABETH: Yes, that's right. *(As HEDDA.)* "There, there! And I'm going to treat you like a friend, as I did before, and call you my dear Thora."

MARION: *(As THEA.)* "Thea."

ELIZABETH: *(As HEDDA.)* "Of course. I meant Thea. You're not accustomed to goodness and kindness, Thea … " That's the way to do it.

MARION: They have a feeling for each other. Very complex and very contradictory. There is affection, and yet there's suspicion and distrust.

ELIZABETH: Yes. There is a violence and a fear between them. They must have been very close once. And one betrayed the other. I feel that Thea betrayed Hedda, and not the other way around; although Hedda seems to be the one who is on top now, the one who is in control. But she's hurt. She feels ... How could this little ... person have thought—that she could ... How dare she. How could she take me for granted, etc. Whatever it is she did do. Which we'll find out when we see more of the script. When we get a few more pages?

MARION: Yes.

ELIZABETH: It's not something rational. I don't think this is about rational people.

MARION: No. I don't think so either.

ELIZABETH: It's about love. And it's about hatred. Love and hatred that are experienced at the same moment. Do you know how difficult that is? Sibling rivalry. Maybe they are sisters. They are sisters. No, they aren't. They met at school. It's a terrible feeling. It's murderous. Overwhelming. *(Pause.)* It should be more physical. That feeling, that fever should be demonstrated physically. There are currents, waves, negative and positive waves, that envelop them. That lift them and push them down and down into the pit and up again. Currents that control them.

MARION: Yes.

ELIZABETH: Let us go.

They get into position. Their movements are now extreme.

ELIZABETH: *(As HEDDA.)* "There! We've killed two birds with one stone."

MARION: *(As THEA.)* "What do you mean?"

ELIZABETH: *(As HEDDA.)* "I wanted to get rid of him."

MARION: *(As THEA.)* " ... So he'd write the letter?"

ELIZABETH: *(As HEDDA.)* "So I'd be able to speak to you."

MARION: *(As THEA.)* "About the same thing?"

ELIZABETH: *(As HEDDA.)* "Yes."

MARION: *(As THEA.)* "But there isn't anything else to say, Mrs. Tesman. Nothing at all."

ELIZABETH: *(As HEDDA.)* "Oh yes there is. There's a lot more—I can see that. Sit here—and we'll have a cozy, confidential chat." *(She takes MARION's hand and brings her to sit next to her.)*

MARION: *(As THEA.)* "But my dear Mrs. Tesman—I should be leaving now."

ELIZABETH: *(As HEDDA.)* "Oh, there's no hurry.— Now, tell me a little about your life at home. For it will all come out anyway!"

MARION: *(As THEA.)* "That is the last thing I care to speak about."

ELIZABETH: *(As HEDDA.)* "Not to me, dear? Weren't we friends at school?"

MARION: *(As THEA.)* "You were one class ahead of me. Oh, I used to be afraid of you."

ELIZABETH: *(As HEDDA.)* "Afraid of me?"

MARION: *(As THEA.)* "Yes, very. You pulled my hair on the stairs."

ELIZABETH: *(As HEDDA.)* "Did I?"

MARION: *(As THEA.)* "Yes, and once you said you would burn the hair off my head."

ELIZABETH: *(As HEDDA.)* "It was only in fun."

MARION: *(As THEA.)* "Yes, but I was very silly in those days.—And since then, anyway, we have drifted so far apart. Our circles have been very different."

ELIZABETH: *(As HEDDA.)* "Well, let's see if we can drift closer together again. At school we used to confide in each other, and we called each other by our first names."

MARION: *(As THEA.)* "Oh no, you're mistaken."

ELIZABETH: *(As HEDDA.)* "'Not at all! I remember very well. So now we are going to renew our friendship.' *(She gets closer to MRS. ELVSTED.)* 'There now!' *(She kisses her cheek.)* 'You must talk to me like a friend and call me Hedda.'" *(HEDDA presses and pats MRS. ELVSTED's hands.)*

MARION: *(As THEA.)* "Oh, you're so kind! I'm not used to this kindness."

ELIZABETH: *(As HEDDA.)* "There, there! And I'm going to treat you like a friend, as I did before, and call you my dear Thora."

MARION: *(As THEA.)* "Thea."

ELIZABETH: *(As HEDDA.)* "Of course. I meant Thea. You're not accustomed to goodness and kindness, Thea … "

MARION: *(As THEA.)* "No."

ELIZABETH: Yes, yes-yes. We all experience that. Don't we?

MARION: What, Elizabeth?

ELIZABETH: We have an interest in disaster, Marion. We take pleasure in it. Don't we? We enjoy seeing someone disintegrate. Yes, that is common enough. Isn't it?

MARION: Really ...

ELIZABETH: Yes, people who are well-meaning and plain can provoke in people who are possessed by a malevolent mischief a desire to poke fun at them. That's what it is. Thea is well-meaning and plain, and she provokes in Hedda a desire to poke fun at her. And so does Tesman provoke that malevolent conduct in her. These people provoke in her a desire to poke fun at them. As if to her they are a different species. To her they are a different species created for her amusement. It is not different from that perverse desire children sometimes have to torture small pests, insects, or a pet.

ELIZABETH: *(Becoming grave. A pause. Dark thoughts.)* She's capable. She has an interesting mind. But she doesn't use it to be constructive. She uses it to be destructive and to complicate her life and the lives of others. How terrible. But, oh, is she interesting. *(Short pause.)* Thea is different. She's kind. She's studious, thoughtful. She's generous. A blessing to one who feels in need of kindness. But she doesn't fascinate us. Of course you do. But she doesn't.

MARION: Thea is different, realistic. She has her feet on the ground. But she's not dull.

ELIZABETH: Oh, no, of course she is not dull. *(Pause.)* They are of course quite incompatible. That's quite clear in this scene. In fact it's quite clear they're headed for disaster.

MARION: Oh, yes.

ELIZABETH: Thea is provincial. But she is smarter than Hedda because she is sensible and she's generous, and Hedda is neither. And that is being smarter, because Hedda uses her brain senselessly. Thea is positive, constructive. Hedda is a person who could do anything she wants to. Don't you think so?

MARION: I don't know.

ELIZABETH: Well, she could. But she doesn't. She is missing a part of herself, and therefore she's missing a part of the world. She is like a person who is colorblind, and therefore is connected to everything but color. When people who are colorblind first learn the words for colors, they do not know what they mean. Then they begin to think that they refer to an abstract quality of the subject. But they don't know what that quality is. They think it may describe something like a mood or a state of being. Until one day someone says, "Pass me the blue ribbon." And someone picks up a specific ribbon and hands it to the person. The colorblind person then understands that color is not an abstract quality, but a specific quality. When a person is colorblind, we who can see color are well aware they can't see color because they use the wrong word when they speak of color. But with other qualities we do not realize when a person is lacking a particular sense or a particular sensitivity to something. Do you know what I mean?

MARION: Heavens, Elizabeth, how in the world are you going to play a character like that?

ELIZABETH: Well, I'll have to work on it.

Scene 5

Two weeks later. VERNON stands behind the high desk repairing a picture frame. At the same time, he is trying to memorize a text from a medical book. There is a folded newspaper on the table. As the lights begin to come up there is a knock on the door. VERNON walks to the door and opens it.

VERNON: Hello, Marion.

MARION: Hello, Vernon. *(She enters. She is downcast.)* Is Elizabeth in?

VERNON: No ... What's the matter?

MARION: Everyone is upset. Elizabeth is upset, Archer is upset, and I'm upset.

VERNON: *(Handing MARION the newspaper.)* Did you see this? Archer accused Gosse of being a traitor translator. He says Gosse's translation is the exercise of a fourth-form schoolboy. He speaks of Gosse's "hopelessly wrong, awkward, silly, and misleading phrases." And there's more. He says that Hedda's burning of Lovborg's manuscript "pales in comparison to what Gosse has done to Ibsen's play." He says, "Hedda obtained the manuscript by chance. Once in her possession, all she did was burn it; while Gosse defaced Ibsen's play. He stultified it, published it, and then claimed copyright."

MARION: It has come to that?

VERNON: Yes. He says Gosse is a man of letters, but not a man of the theatre. And he is not a capable translator of Norwegian. He says Gosse has totally mangled the original. And that McArthy is further destroying the play with his cheap Anglicized adaptation and direction. And what's even worse, he says, "They're even cutting sections of the play because La Langtry cannot do them."

MARION: Goodness.

VERNON: Because—she cannot—do them.

MARION: *(In disbelief.)* They—are—cutting—parts—of—the—play—because—she—cannot—do—them?

VERNON: Because she cannot do them.

MARION: Cannot do them.

VERNON: That's what I've heard.

There's a knock at the door. VERNON goes to the door.

VERNON: That must be David.

MARION: Who's David?

VERNON: David. Don't you know David?

MARION: Will he be in the play?

VERNON: I don't know.

There is another knock on the door. VERNON opens the door.

VERNON: Hi, David. I'm Vernon, Elizabeth's brother.

DAVID: Hello. Am I late?

VERNON: You're not late. Marion and I were just talking.

DAVID enters. He carries a briefcase and some folders.

VERNON: You know Marion?

DAVID gasps.

VERNON: *(Indicating one, then the other.)* Marion. David.

DAVID: *(Going to her.)* ... Marion Lea ... *(Going on his knees.)* I've seen you on the stage, Miss Lea. I am an admirer of your work.

MARION: Oh, thank you.

DAVID: I saw you in *The Sixth Commandment.*

MARION: Oh.

DAVID: You were wonderful.

MARION: Thank you.

DAVID *puts his head to the floor.*

VERNON: *(Indicating a chair.)* Sit down, David. You want something to drink? Tea?

DAVID: Yes, tea. *(Starts to stand.)* I'll make it.

VERNON: That's all right. I just put water on.

DAVID *sits.*

VERNON: Marion and I were just talking about the Archer-Gosse debate.

DAVID: What is it?

VERNON: It seems that the rights to the play that we want to do have been acquired, and the translator does not have Norwegian.

The tea kettle whistles. VERNON *continues speaking as he exits and prepares the tea offstage.*

DAVID: Is that the translation we're going to use?

VERNON: Are you going to be in the play?

DAVID: Am I not?

VERNON: I don't know. We don't know what parts there are.

DAVID: You don't?

VERNON: We haven't read the play.

DAVID: You haven't?

VERNON: We haven't seen a copy yet.

DAVID: Oh, I see.

VERNON: You want milk? Sugar?

DAVID: Milk, please.

VERNON goes to the kitchen.

DAVID: Are you in the play?

MARION: Yes.

DAVID: What part are you playing?

MARION: Thea Elvsted.

DAVID: Have you read it?

MARION: The play?

DAVID: Yes.

MARION: Only a few pages.

DAVID: Hmm. Are there any parts for men?

MARION: There's one I know of for sure.

DAVID: Who's that?

MARION: Tesman.

DAVID: Who's that?

MARION: He seems to be a relative.

DAVID: Is this a good part?

MARION: I don't know. He went off to write a letter. And she told him to be cordial in the letter.

DAVID: I see. Anything else?

MARION: Hedda was glad to get rid of him.

DAVID: Is he not an interesting person?

MARION: Not to Hedda. She wanted to talk to me.

DAVID: What about?

MARION: I didn't quite understand.

DAVID: I see. Is Ibsen in the play?

MARION: Ibsen wrote the play.

DAVID: Yes. But he is in the play?

MARION: What made you think that?

DAVID: Someone said to me I was playing Ibsen.

MARION: Who said that?

DAVID: Elizabeth told a friend of mine that she wanted me to be in the play and that she wanted me to play Ibsen, and that I should come here and meet with her.

MARION: I see.

DAVID: Hmm. Miss Lea, in particular I admire the moment ... *(Reproducing MARION's movements.)* when, with your head bowed, you went from stage left to the window to the right, reached the frame of the window, and there, lifted your head slowly. Then you lifted your right hand to your brow. And, slowly, you lowered your head again ever so gently as the lights faded, and ahhh ... the curtains closed. *(He closes his eyes to retain the image a moment longer.)*

MARION: Oh, ... you're so kind ...

DAVID: It's not kindness, Miss Lea.

MARION: Oh, it is.

DAVID: No, it isn't, Miss Lea.

VERNON: *(Entering. He brings a cup of tea. He places the cup of tea on the table.)* Here you are, David, this is your tea.

DAVID: Thank you. While we wait, may I show you some of the things I've found that may be of relevance to the subject of interest? I was looking in the library at papers, letters, clippings and other writings of Mr. Ibsen. And I was also looking at other things under the subject of psychology. Because I think that his plays show an interest in and understanding of the human psyche, deeper than other authors. Ibsen is also interested in the subject of power, of seduction and submission and the possession of another, and in other subjects of human and social dimension.

VERNON: Yes. A play is not simply a story that's being told. *(DAVID and MARION look at him.)* Yes. Nor is it simply a means for the writer to say something he wishes to say. *(Short pause.)* No. A friend of Sven's, a playwright, was talking to Sven and me about writing. Plays. She's written a few. She said that a play is a riddle. A riddle that's in the head of the author. *(PAUSE.)* Something that intrigues the author but doesn't have a shape yet. It doesn't even have a question. And a riddle, of course, must have a question. The question is an important part of the riddle. How can you have a riddle without a question? She says that, in the beginning, all the author has is that there is something to be discovered. That is all she has. And the writing of the play is its discovery. She says that by the time the author gets halfway through, she knows what the question is. Then, answering the question begins to shape the play. She says every answer creates another question. And each answer makes the play grow. When the questions begin to dwindle, that means the play is coming to an end. The last question is the one whose answer doesn't invite another question. At the start, the subject haunts the writer. And at the end, the writer is in a state of bliss. Do you think that's right?

DAVID: That sounds right.

VERNON: So, you see. When the play is to be performed, first one must examine it, not unlike how a doctor examines a patient. One must understand its nature and learn how it evolves from one moment to the next. A play has a nature like any other living thing, and to bring it to life one must understand its nature. *(Pause.)* I'm going on an errand. See you later.

MARION: So long, Vernon.

DAVID: Thoughtful young man.

VERNON: So long, David.

DAVID: Oh. So long, Vernon.

DAVID takes a folder and book out of his satchel. VERNON goes to the door and opens it. LADY BELL is standing outside the door with her fist raised about to knock. Both VERNON and LADY BELL jump and let out a scream. DAVID tastes the tea, makes a face, and puts the cup down.

VERNON: Oh! Lady Bell!

MARION: He put sugar in it?

DAVID: That's all right, Miss Lea.

LADY BELL: Oh. You scared me! Oh!

MARION: You don't take sugar?

DAVID: ... No.

VERNON: I'm sorry. I was just going out.

MARION: I'm sorry. *(Reaches for the cup.)* I'll make you another cup.

LADY BELL: *(Apologetic.)* I was about to knock.

DAVID: It's all right. I don't mind.

VERNON: Come in, Lady Bell.

MARION: *(Picking up the cup.)* I'll make you a fresh cup.

LADY BELL: The door just opened and I ...

DAVID: *(Going after MARION.)* I can drink it like this.

VERNON: I'm sorry I scared you.

DAVID: I don't mind the sugar.

LADY BELL: No. I thought I scared you.

MARION takes the cup from him and starts toward the kitchen. DAVID tries to block her way.

DAVID: I like it with sugar!

VERNON: Are you all right, Lady Bell?

MARION: No you don't.

LADY BELL: Just a momentary fright.

DAVID: *(Sits down and puts his head on his hands.)* Oh my God. What have I done?

VERNON: Welcome, Lady Bell.

MARION: You have done nothing!

LADY BELL: What is this?

DAVID: *(Weeping.)* Oh my God!

VERNON: *(There is a moment's pause. VERNON leads LADY BELL in.)* Are you alright, David?

DAVID: Yes.

VERNON: Lady Bell, this is David. David, Lady Bell.

LADY BELL: How do you do.

DAVID: How do you do.

LADY BELL: It's a great pleasure to meet you.

VERNON: Sit down, Lady Bell. Where would you like to sit?

LADY BELL: Here, I would like to sit here. *(She sits.)*

DAVID *throws himself on his knees, his head on the floor at* LADY BELL's *feet.*

MARION: This is David, Lady Bell.

LADY BELL: How do you do, David.

DAVID: How do you do, Lady Bell. I am an admirer of your work.

LADY BELL: Thank you, David. Why are you on your knees?

MARION: Well, David was telling me about some letters and other things he has found about the play we are going to do.

LADY BELL: Oh? Go ahead, David, I am eager to learn whatever there is to know about it.

DAVID: We're going to do Henrik Ibsen's latest play. It is entitled *Hedda Gabler.*

LADY BELL: Oh yes! Elizabeth is the happiest person in her hope of doing Henrik Ibsen's latest oeuvre.

MARION: David was going to show us some papers, letters, and clippings he has found.

LADY BELL: Oh yes. I am sure everyone is eager to see them. Tell us what you have found.

DAVID: Yes. The play is possibly about detachment and about devouring desires. I think that subject is quite interesting. Don't you think it is about devouring desires?

LADY BELL: Oh yes, David!

DAVID *takes out some sheets of paper from the folder.*

DAVID: I know a person who has had correspondence with Ibsen. And has let me have copies of notes he made from his correspondence with him and also notes he made of conversations with him. May I read some of this to you?

MARION: Of course.

DAVID *is about to read.*

MARION: Wait!

VERNON: What?

MARION: We must wait for Elizabeth!

VERNON: That's right.

MARION: Oh, I hope that's Elizabeth. *(The door opens and ELIZABETH enters, preoccupied.)* Thank God Elizabeth has arrived, because I don't think I could have waited very long.

ELIZABETH paces all around the room.

ELIZABETH: Good morning, Marion.

MARION: *(Bows.)* Good morning, Elizabeth.

ELIZABETH: *(Turns to VERNON.)* Hello, Vernon. *(VERNON bows and exits. As ELIZABETH paces by LADY BELL, she stops for a moment.)* Hello, Lady Bell, I am so glad to see you. *(They bow to each other, ELIZABETH kisses her on the cheek and continues pacing. ELIZABETH goes to the settee and throws herself on it. A moment later, DAVID rushes to the side of the settee, throws himself on his knees, and bows his head. ELIZABETH turns her head to look at him. Without raising his head, DAVID raises the sheet he has in his hand and offers it to her.)* What is this? What is this? What is this? *(Reading.)* "While having lunch with Ibsen, his friend and doctor heard him say: 'My next work,— My next work, my next work—*Hedda Gabler*—is hovering before me. Something I see clearly.—An experience I, myself, had with a very young woman.'" A young woman. A young woman. A young woman. "'A very interesting Viennese girl I met in Gossensass—a summer when I was alone, away from my family, working on a new play. This girl had remarkable qualities, remarkable qualities, and she confided a great number of things to me. She told me things that were extraordinary. Once she said, 'I am not interested in marrying a decently brought-up man. What interests me is to lure a married man away from his wife. To take a married woman's husband from her.' And Ibsen added: ... 'She was a demonic little wrecker.—Like a bird of prey. She would gladly have included me among her victims. But she had no great success. She wanted to possess me. But instead, I possessed her. For! My! Play! The little Viennese wrecker's name was Emilie Bardach.'" For his play. For his play. For his play. *(She stands and paces. She pants. She goes to DAVID, who is still on the floor.)*

MARION: That is she.

DAVID: Who?

MARION: That is she.

ELIZABETH. Who?

MARION: That is she.

ELIZABETH: Who is that girl? What is she like? … Where is she?

MARION: That is she. That is she.

DAVID: Who? Who?

MARION: Hedda Gabler. Hedda Gabler. Don't you see? That girl is Hedda Gabler.

DAVID: She's beautiful. Unusual face. Like a cat. Her eyes are yellow. Her eyelids move slowly. She blinks. You look. She waits. She breathes. Her eyes close. You look at her chest heave. She breathes again. She speaks. You look. She waits. You're at her mercy, at her feet. She speaks fast, you get dizzy. She puts her teeth in your neck. You want to touch her. No need to say any more. That's what Hedda is like. She looks like a saint, but beware. She's not. She's very interesting.

ELIZABETH *walks down to them. She sits.*

ELIZABETH: And Ibsen? What is he like?

DAVID: … He's old … Strong … Physically strong … Mentally strong … He's passionate … Stubborn. Suspicious and cautious. Yet he's trusting, naïve. He is rigid. There is an impotent side to him, and a side where he is unfathomable. He is on fire. He leads many lives in his mind. He feels a sword will be put through him and crack a hole in him. He's made of glass. He is a coward. As a man he is a coward. As a writer he is courageous. Courageous! He delves into delicate, mysterious, and dangerous things. *(Short pause.)* I'm glad I'm going to be playing this part.

MARION: What part is that?

DAVID: Ibsen.

MARION: Is Ibsen in the play?

DAVID: Isn't he?

MARION: I don't know.

DAVID: Oh, well, I hope he is … Because how often does one have the chance to play the part of a man who is possessed by a demon? Who retaliates aggressively but submits and is possessed. And acts cowardly and doesn't admit to it. That will be interesting! What an opportunity! Because how often does one have the chance to be possessed by someone else?

MARION: By this woman?

DAVID: Yes ... or destroyed.

MARION: It would interest you to be destroyed?

DAVID: Yes. That is how you are reborn. You die and then you are reborn. How often does one have the opportunity to experience being possessed by someone else? Owned by someone else! Be it a demon or not. An angel or a beast. Owned by a demon, or an angel, or a beast. Be owned. Be possessed.

LADY BELL: Yes, yes, yes!

MARION: By this woman?

DAVID: Yes.

MARION: Or destroyed?

LADY BELL: Yes!

DAVID: That's how you're reborn.

MARION: Reborn?

LADY BELL: Yes!

Short pause.

MARION: And returned to life.

LADY BELL: As someone else.

DAVID: As yourself ... reborn ... wiser ... with ten hearts!

LADY BELL: You have an interesting mind, David.

MARION: Yes!

ELIZABETH: Yes!

LADY BELL: Yes!

DAVID: Yes!

MARION: I hope there is a part for you in this play. It will be wonderful to work with you, David.

DAVID: Thank you. Now, I understand in this play there's also a character of a woman who is a gambler. Who will play that? I have never played the role of a woman, but without any doubt I could pass for a woman if I could get the right wig and a dress made for me. Unless you know a tall woman who has a dress that a woman such as Hedda would wear, and she wouldn't mind lending it to us for the production.

MARION: What makes you think there is a gambler?

DAVID: I believe Ibsen has written about gambling as a natural although unusual instinct in mankind. More common among men, but women have a more intense, although secret, yet untapped gambling instinct. In a sense, something like a religious drive—an urge to stand on a line so fine, a tightrope that lifts upwards and upwards ever further, higher and higher. In a state of balance so perilous, and yet so consuming, that rather than wish for safety, one is greedy for more height, more distance from the land. More at risk of death, and yet attracted to the ascension, while fearing the fall. Being pulled to more height, and yet in horror, attracted to the fall. That vertigo is what a gambler feels at that moment when he has put all his chips on one number, the roulette is turning, the click click click click click sound speeds up, then it starts to approach the end. Omnipotence. The moment of bliss. —A deal.

Lights fade, then slowly come up.

ELIZABETH: "Here I sit as usual at my desk, and would gladly work,"—Ibsen—"and would gladly work, but cannot."—To Emilie—"My imagination is raging, but it strays where it should not. I cannot keep down the memory of summer, nor do I want to. The things we have lived through I live again and again and still again. Once we talked about Stupidity and Madness, and you remarked, in your soft, musical voice, and with your faraway look, that there is a difference between Stupidity and Madness ... Well then, I keep thinking over and over again: Was it stupidity or was it madness that we should have come together? Or was it both stupidity and madness? Or was it neither? It was a simple necessity of nature. It was also our fate." Oh, Marion. Oh yes, I know. Oh Lady Bell, I know. Thank you, David.

MARION: *(Reading.)* "He is a volcano! So terribly beautiful.—Passion comes to me when it cannot lead to anything." She wrote this. "Eternal obstacles. This! And only this! Is true love! But oh, how sad I feel ... for he fears his love for me" ... *(She looks up.)* ... Oh, Elizabeth. Lady Bell. It is so beautiful.

VERNON enters. He holds a package behind him. Sings fanfare.

VERNON: Guess what I have in my hands.

There is silence.

ELIZABETH: What, Vernon?

VERNON: Guess.

ELIZABETH: *(Breathless.)* What is it?

Vernon shows a package.

VERNON: Fresh off the press.—In English!

They step towards VERNON as they emit a profound sigh.

Scene 6

VERNON sits on the platform center right. He is fixing his camera. LADY BELL sits to the left. She is reading.

VERNON: One would think that medicine has nothing to do with art. But it does. The most important thing in medicine is diagnosis. Isn't it?

LADY BELL: Is it, Vernon?

VERNON: Oh, yes.—Of course. If a new patient were not first diagnosed and then treated properly, he could not recover.

LADY BELL: He couldn't, could he?

VERNON: No, he couldn't.

LADY BELL: He would die then. Wouldn't he?

VERNON: Yes, he would. Unless his own constitution comes to his rescue.

LADY BELL: And saves him.

VERNON: Yes.

LADY BELL: What a relief. For him and for his family.

VERNON: Yes.—Of course, there are illnesses from which no one has ever recovered, even with treatment.

LADY BELL: What do you mean?

VERNON: I mean that there are illnesses that, even after treatment, can cause a patient's death. Diseases for which there is no cure.

LADY BELL: Incurable diseases.

VERNON: Yes. And there are diseases that require early treatment.

LADY BELL: Yes. Diseases which must be recognized and treated at an early stage if the patient is to survive.

VERNON: *(Short pause.)* People also die of old age.

LADY BELL: *(Short pause.)* How do you diagnose old age?

VERNON: Oh, Lady Bell.

LADY BELL: I mean, can they determine the reasons for it?

VERNON: Well ... the reason for it is time ... Time is what causes old age.

LADY BELL: *(Short pause.)* Isn't that odd. And there's no treatment for it.

VERNON: No, not until we learn to do away with time.

LADY BELL: Oh, no, Vernon, time is one of the best things we have.

VERNON: *(Laughing.)* Oh, Lady Bell.

LADY BELL: And I'm good at doing things with it.

VERNON: Yes, you are. You can do all kinds of things with it. We can all learn from you.

LADY BELL: Yes, Vernon, I'm sure you're going to be a very fine doctor.

Scene 7

Opening night. VERNON and DAVID are at ELIZABETH's apartment.

VERNON: Well, this is it. This is the night.

DAVID: You mean the opening?

VERNON: That's what we call opening night. We say the night.

DAVID: I see.

VERNON: It's going to be good.

DAVID: I'm sure.

VERNON: Everyone has their lines down.

DAVID: Good. If not it would lack veracity.

VERNON: Yes. Although having the lines down is not all that matters.

DAVID: No?

VERNON: The hardest part is finding the character within oneself.

DAVID: You mean one has to find the character within oneself?

VERNON: I think so.

DAVID: May one not find it outside oneself?

VERNON: Elizabeth says one ought to find it within.

DAVID: Well, she ought to know.

VERNON: Even if you're playing a horrible person.

DAVID: *(Imagining the process.)* I see. That could be troubling. Don't you agree?

VERNON: Yes. Elizabeth says yes. When she's rehearsing, sometimes she behaves strangely—she says it can be troubling. But then, it's not. She says in performance it's not painful. Except sometimes.

DAVID: Yes. I can see how finding the character within oneself could inspire a performance of greater magnitude. However, there are things that are not part of our existence, but are outside ourselves, like imitation, which could also be of great value to creation.

VERNON: How would you play a horrible person?

DAVID: Well, I would say you have to study the character of a horrible person. I have files on a number of them.

VERNON: If I were an actor, I would like to play characters who are good-natured, personable, and constructive.

DAVID: I don't think that's the best choice, Vernon. In real life one wants to associate with people who are good-natured and personable. But on stage such people are not the best choice.

VERNON: Why not, David?

DAVID: On stage the most interesting characters are the ones who make life difficult for everyone else.

VERNON: I see. Well, the play is good so I don't see how it could possibly not be a success. And even if they don't like the play, they have to like the actors. I heard tonight is sold out. Is that so?

DAVID: It's sold out. All the London intelligentsia are going to be there. Henry James is coming. Bernard Shaw is coming. Oscar Wilde, William Archer are coming. Everyone is going to be there. Everyone is excited. Some people object to the content of the play. But those are only philistines who have no understanding of great modern drama. None of them would say that *Medea* is filth, or *Othello*, or even *Hamlet*. Or they wouldn't dare say it even if they thought it was. And besides, every good play has some filth.

Scene 8

The stage curtains are drawn. LADY BELL and DAVID enter. They go center stage. There is a spot on them.

DAVID: Ladies and Gentlemen. As prologue to the English premiere of Henrik Ibsen's masterpiece, we will perform our new work entitled *Norwegian Elegy*.

They signal for the music to start; then dance a German Expressionist piece.

Scene 9

TESMAN (VERNON) and MRS. ELVSTED (MARION) are on the floor sorting out pages of LOVBORG's manuscript. BRACK (DAVID) watches them. HEDDA (ELIZABETH) starts downstage left and watches them.

HEDDA: So I'm in your power, Judge Brack. From now on you have a hold on me.

BRACK: Dearest Hedda—believe me—I shall not abuse my advantage.

HEDDA: Nonetheless, I am in your power. At the mercy of your will and demands. A slave! I can't endure that! I won't submit to that!

BRACK: It's inevitable.

HEDDA: You think so? *(She walks down and to the side of MRS. ELVSTED and TESMAN.)* Well? Are you getting on, Jorgen? Eh?

TESMAN: Heaven knows, dear. In any case it will be the work of months.

HEDDA: *(As before.)* Fancy that! *(She passes her hand softly through MRS. ELVSTED's hair.)* Doesn't it seem strange to you, Thea? Here you are sitting with Tesman—just as you sat with Ejlert Lovborg?

MRS. ELVSTED: Ah, if I could only inspire your husband the way I did him?

HEDDA: Oh, it will come—in time.

TESMAN: Yes, do you know, Hedda—I really think I begin to feel something of the sort. But won't you go and sit with Brack again?

HEDDA: Is there nothing I can help you with?

TESMAN: No, nothing in the world. *(Turning his head.)* I trust you to keep Hedda company, my dear Brack.

BRACK: *(With a glance at HEDDA.)* With the very greatest of pleasure.

HEDDA: Thanks, dear. But I'm tired this evening. I think I'll go and lie down.

TESMAN: Yes, do,—eh?

HEDDA goes into the back room and draws the curtains. A short pause. Suddenly she is heard playing a wild dance on the piano. TESMAN goes to the curtain and moves it slightly to talk to HEDDA.

TESMAN: Hedda.—Hedda.—My dearest Hedda—don't play the piano.

Hedda: *(Offstage, as she plays.)* And of Aunt Julle. And of all the rest of them.—After this, I will be quiet.

TESMAN: *(Returning to the papers.)* It upsets her to see us at this sad task. I'll tell you what, Mrs. Elvsted.—You shall take the empty room at Aunt Julle's, and then I will come over in the evenings, and we can sit and work there—eh?

MRS. ELVSTED: Yes, that would be best.

HEDDA: I hear what you're saying, Tesman. But how am I going to get through the evenings here by myself?

TESMAN: Oh, I dare say Judge Brack will be so kind as to look in now and then, even though I am out.

BRACK: Willingly! Every blessed evening, Mrs. Tesman! We shall get along very well.

HEDDA: *(Speaking loud and clear.)* You're looking forward to that, Judge Brack? Now that you're the only cock in the yard.

A shot is heard within. TESMAN, MRS. ELVSTED, and BRACK leap to their feet as TESMAN speaks.

TESMAN: She's playing with those pistols again. *(TESMAN opens the curtains.)* Shot herself! Shot herself in the temple! Imagine that!

BRACK: *(Very grave.)* Good God!—People don't do such things!

The actors take their bows. As the other actors take a second bow, ELIZABETH walks forward. She holds a paper and reads.

Scene 10

ELIZABETH: *(Reading.)* "The reason why I'm here this evening to speak before the Royal Society of Arts on this Twelfth of March 1928, is to …"

As the lights begin to fade slowly, music starts almost inaudibly and continues to increase in volume, as the volume of ELIZABETH's voice decreases.

ELIZABETH: *(Reading.)* " … speak to you of the significance of Henrik Ibsen for those who have attended performances of his plays, and those fortunate enough to have performed in them—in short, all those whose lives have been changed by the work of the great Norwegian. And most importantly, for the women among them. Naturally I'm thinking of the first performance of *A Doll's House* in the English language and the actress, Janet Achurch, to whom belongs the lasting honor of being the first to perform Nora, the great Ibsen part. Those who were present, Marion Lea, …"

ELIZABETH's voice is inaudible. She is now mouthing the words. The volume of the music increases.

ELIZABETH: *(Reading.)*: " … myself, and many others were to be affected by that evening's event for the rest of our lives."

She is now mouthing words as the lights fade out.

What of the Night?

* * * * * * * * * * * * *

"Watchman, what of the night?"
The watchman said, "The morning cometh and also the night."

ISAIAH 21.11–12

What of the Night? consists of four separate plays. The earlier plays were *Nadine*, originally titled *The Mother*s when presented at the Padua Hills Festival, Los Angeles, California, 1986 (later called *Charlie* at the Milwaukee Repertory Theater), and *Hunger*, produced by Engarde Arts, New York City, 1988. *Springtime* and *Lust* were added to them for the final version, entitled *And What Of The Night?*, which premiered at the Milwaukee Repertory Theater, Milwaukee, Wisconsin, March 4, 1989.

CASTS

FOR *NADINE:*

NADINE/REBA, Marilyn Frank
CHARLIE, Steven J. Gefroh
PETE, Daniel Mooney
LEAH, Marie Mathay
RAINBOW, Kelly Maurer
BIRDIE, Catherine Lynn Davis
JOE, Steven Folstein
PANHANDLERS:
    Nomi Bence
    Larry Dean Birkett
    Terrance P. Flynn
    Steven Folstein
    Cynthia Hewett
    Heather Kendall
    Amy Malloy
    Joan Rater
    Holly Smith

FOR *SPRINGTIME:*

GRETA, Catherine Lynn Davis
RAINBOW, Kelly Maurer
RAY, Daniel Mooney

FOR *LUST:*

RAY, Daniel Mooney
JOSEPH, Kenneth Albers
HELENA, Marie Mathay
JIM, Larry Dean Birkett
SHE, Catherine Lynn Davis
LORRAINE, Kelly Maurer
WANG, Steven J. Gefroh
GIRL, Amy Malloy
WING, Marilyn Frank
BOY, Larry Dean Birkett
CROWS:
    Steven Folstein
    Terrance P. Flynn
BIRDIE, Catherine Lynn Davis

FOR *HUNGER:*

CHARLIE, Kenneth Albers
BIRDIE, Catherine Lynn Davis
RAY, Daniel Mooney
REBA, Marilyn Frank
ANGEL, Thomas Van Voorhees

Maria Irene Fornes, *Director*

Cecelia Mason, *Costume Designer*
LeRoy Stoner, *Lighting Designer*
John Story, *Set Designer*

Nadine

CHARACTERS

NADINE: Thirty-five years old. A gaunt, wiry woman. She is tough and practical.
CHARLIE: Sixteen years old. Innocent, gentle, streetwise.
RAINBOW: Nine years old. High-strung and sensitive.
BIRDIE: Fourteen years old. Tough. Streetwise.
LEAH: Thirty-five years old. NADINE's friend.
PETE: Forty years old. Stupid and mean.

In an economically depressed place in the Southwest. 1938.

An empty lot. In back is a sunny sky with billowing clouds. Upstage, from right to left, is a sideboard, a bassinet, a rocking chair, and a tree. On top of the sideboard there is a basin with water and some statues of saints. Center right there is a dining table with four chairs. On the left there is a mattress on the floor.

Scene 1

A live singer or a recording of Patsy Cline's "Leaving on Your Mind." As the lights come up, the music fades. PETE sits on a chair that has been placed to the left. CHARLIE stands by the table. He wears a pair of pants and a tattered shirt. He is barefoot. PETE wears a frayed suit and hat. He wears shoes.

PETE: Did you get some stuff?

CHARLIE: Yeah.

PETE: Let's see.

CHARLIE: What?

PETE: The stuff, Charlie.

CHARLIE goes to the sideboard and takes out a cardboard box that contains clothing, empty cans, bottles, books, magazines, and other objects. He takes the box to PETE. PETE examines the contents of the box with disdain.

PETE: This is not good, Charlie.—You can throw that stuff out. *(Pause.)* I heard you got some good stuff.

CHARLIE looks down.

PETE: So?

CHARLIE: That's it, Pete.

PETE: Oh, yeah?

CHARLIE: ... Yeah ...

PETE *gives* CHARLIE *a knowing look.*

CHARLIE: I got some other stuff.

PETE: That's what I said. Bring it out.

CHARLIE: It's not that good.

PETE: Bring it out.

CHARLIE: I thought I could keep some.

PETE: How come?

CHARLIE: I thought I could.

PETE: Who told you that?

CHARLIE: Maybe you did, Pete.

PETE: Never said that.

CHARLIE: Oh.

PETE: Better get it, Charlie.

CHARLIE: Yeah. *(He goes to the sideboard, gets a paper bag full of clothes, and puts it on the floor.)* Here it is, Pete.

PETE: What's here?

CHARLIE: You can see for yourself, Pete.—It's not good.

PETE: Let's see.

CHARLIE: It's no good, Pete.

PETE *goes to* CHARLIE *and sends him flying with a punch in the jaw.*

PETE: Show me, Charlie.

CHARLIE'S *mouth is bleeding. He crawls to the bag. He takes out a garment.*

PETE: What's that?

CHARLIE: A jacket.

PETE: Is it good?

CHARLIE: It's torn.

PETE: Did you do that?

CHARLIE: No, Pete.

PETE shows CHARLIE a fist.

CHARLIE: Pulled it off him.

As PETE punches CHARLIE in the face.

CHARLIE: No, Pete!

PETE: I said, don't be rough with the clothes. *(Pause.)* What do you say?

CHARLIE: Yeah, Pete.

PETE: I said to be careful.—What else?

CHARLIE: *(Pulling out a pair of pants.)* Pants.

PETE: Let's see.

CHARLIE hands PETE the pants. PETE looks at the pants. Then he looks at the pants CHARLIE is wearing.

PETE: Take them off.

CHARLIE: Pete.

PETE: Take them off.

CHARLIE takes off his pants and hands them to PETE. PETE puts the pants on the pile.

PETE: What else?

CHARLIE: There's a shirt.

PETE: *(Pointing to the pile.)* Put it here.

CHARLIE does.

PETE: Underwear?

102 ● MARIA IRENE FORNES

CHARLIE: Yes.

PETE: Let's see.

CHARLIE slides the bag towards PETE. PETE pushes the bag back with his foot.

PETE: Take it out.

CHARLIE takes out an undershirt and hands it to PETE.

PETE: Undershirt?

CHARLIE: Yes.

PETE: Put it here.

CHARLIE does.

PETE: What else?

CHARLIE takes out a pair of socks and puts it in the pile.

CHARLIE: Socks.

Pete: Are they clean?

CHARLIE: No.

PETE: *(Throwing them back at CHARLIE.)* Wash them!—Shorts?

CHARLIE: No.

PETE: How come?

CHARLIE: I left him that.

PETE: How come?

CHARLIE: He was cold.

PETE: He was cold.

CHARLIE: Yeah.

PETE: Was they yours to give?

CHARLIE doesn't answer.

PETE: Was they yours to give!

CHARLIE doesn't answer.

PETE: Was they yours to give!

CHARLIE doesn't answer. PETE punches CHARLIE. CHARLIE falls to the ground. PETE kicks him repeatedly and continues repeating the line through the following speech.

CHARLIE: *(Crying.)* He was naked! I didn't want to leave him naked! He was cold! I felt sorry for him! To be lying in the street cold and hurt. I wouldn't want it done to me! I wouldn't want it done to me! I wouldn't want it done to me! I wouldn't want it done to me!

PETE: Put the stuff in the bag.

CHARLIE starts putting the clothes in the bag.

PETE: This is junk. You hear! Get better stuff or you're out! You hear! I try to place this stuff and it's crap.—You hear! Can't carry you anymore. Shape up or you're out! I want good clothes. You mug bums! I want good stuff! Wallets with money! How come there's never any money? Wristwatches. Don't mug bums, idiot.—And if you ever keep something again, you're dead! You hear! *(He takes the bag and starts to go.)*

CHARLIE: You didn't pay me, Pete.

PETE stops.

PETE: For what?

CHARLIE: For the stuff.

PETE walks to CHARLIE. He stretches his closed hand to him. CHARLIE reaches out. PETE grabs CHARLIE's hand and twists it.

PETE: You want to get paid?

CHARLIE lets out a scream.

CHARLIE: I need some money, Pete.

PETE presses harder on CHARLIE's wrist.

CHARLIE: For Lucille, Pete.

PETE presses harder.

CHARLIE: She needs medicine.

PETE: *(Pressing.)* You want money?

CHARLIE: Oh!

PETE: For what, Charlie? For this junk?

NADINE enters. PETE sees her and releases CHARLIE's hand. She gives him a hard look.

PETE: He's stealing from me.

NADINE: Are you stealing from him, Charlie?

CHARLIE: No.

NADINE: He's not stealing from you. *(To Charlie.)* Did he hurt you?

CHARLIE: Yeah. *(Showing Nadine his hand.)* Look.

NADINE: I don't want you to be hurting the kid.

PETE: He's stealing from me.

NADINE: Okay, you don't hit him. He don't steal from you.

PETE: Okay. *(He starts to go.)*

NADINE: You paid for the clothes?

PETE: No.

NADINE: Why not?

PETE: He tried to steal them.

NADINE: Yeah, but he didn't. So pay.

PETE: Says who, Nadine?

NADINE: Fair's fair.

PETE takes some coins from his pocket and throws them to CHARLIE. He exits. NADINE takes a few steps after PETE.

NADINE: Come back here, Pete. I have to talk to you. Get lost, Charlie. I want to talk to Pete.

PETE reenters.

NADINE: Sit down.

PETE sits.

NADINE: I just thought I'd discuss something with you.

PETE *waits.*

NADINE: I think Charlie should get a bigger cut.

PETE: Who do you think you are, Nadine?

NADINE: I'm Charlie's mother.—And I have to look after him.

PETE: *(Starting to go.)* You don't say.

NADINE: Sit down.

PETE *sits.* NADINE *sits. She tries to be sociable.*

NADINE: I've lost the habit of talking to grownups. You get a little rough screaming at kids all the time. You forget to be civilized.—How about discussing something, Pete? Just sitting down and discussing something with another person. *(She waits.)* I have a sick kid, Pete. She's very sick. She's going to die. And I wanted to know if you ever had a kid. *(She waits.)* Have you ever had kids? *(She waits.)* Lost the habit of talking to grownups, didn't you.—Haven't you, Pete?

PETE *stares at her.*

NADINE: Well, I wonder if you could lend me some money. I could buy some medicine for Lucille. And I could pay you back. *(She waits.)* Pete. *(She waits. A moment passes.)*

CHARLIE *peeks in.*

NADINE: Scram!

CHARLIE *exits.*

NADINE: Charlie goes out every day and risks his skin to get stuff for you. Sometimes he hasn't had a hot meal in days, and you give him pennies for a full day's work even when you know he could get hurt—or arrested—for doing your dirty work. He doesn't ask so much, but he needs more, and you have to give him more. His kid sister's sick, and she has to get medicine. Otherwise she's going to die. You're a nice man. You have a heart.—Give me the money for the medicine.—It's not that much.—You won't let the kid die. *(She waits.)* Pete? *(She waits. She swings at him and misses. She reaches over and grabs him by his shirt collar.)* I'm getting that money one way or another, Pete.

There's a pause. She releases him. She fixes his collar.

PETE: You're funny. *(He starts to stand.)*

NADINE: Sit.

PETE sits. RAINBOW and BIRDIE enter left.

NADINE: What do you want?

There's a pause. RAINBOW and BIRDIE exit. NADINE walks behind PETE. She puts her hand inside his jacket and squeezes his breast. He grabs her arm to remove it but begins to shake. His eyes roll. She lowers her hand to his crotch. He quivers. He pants and grunts. His eyes roll.

NADINE: You got to pay.

PETE shakes his head as he lets air out of his mouth.

NADINE: You gotta.

PETE shakes his head. NADINE grabs his hair and pulls his head back.

NADINE: You gotta.

PETE whimpers and stamps his feet. He growls and drools.

NADINE: You want some?

PETE: Yeah! Yeah!

NADINE: You got to pay!

PETE: No!

NADINE: You got to pay!

PETE: No!

NADINE: You got to pay!

PETE: No!

NADINE: Yeah!

PETE: No!

NADINE: Yeah!

PETE: No!

NADINE: *(Taking her hand off.)* You get none!

PETE snorts, pants, and makes noises as if he is having a heart attack. He puts a dollar on the table. NADINE takes the dollar and puts it in her cleavage.

NADINE: More, Pete! Get it out.

PETE reaches for his fly.

NADINE: *Money!*

PETE puts another dollar on the table. NADINE puts it in her cleavage. He stands and pushes his pelvis against her.

NADINE: More!

PETE puts a dollar in her cleavage. The lights fade as PETE moves his pelvis against NADINE.

PETE: Yeah! *(Moving his pelvis against her.)* Now! Now! Now! *(He pants.)* Now! Now! Now!

Scene 2

CHARLIE wears a pair of very large white pants over his own pants. LEAH sits to the left pinning the back of the pants. BIRDIE sits on the mattress sewing on a veil made from a black crinoline petticoat. She wears bright blue lipstick. RAINBOW sits next to her. She reads a comic. NADINE sits in the rocker. She holds LUCILLE, wrapped in a blanket, in her arms.

CHARLIE: *(Pulling the pants out at the waist.)* They're too big, Mom.

NADINE: Take the other pants off, Charlie. You can't wear two pairs of pants at the same time and expect them to fit.—I hope your kids are smarter than mine, Leah.

LEAH: They're not any smarter. Kids are not smart nowadays.

CHARLIE: *(To LEAH.)* I don't see why you think you're so smart. You old folks always think you're smart.

LEAH: *(Turning CHARLIE around to pin the front of his pants.)* I'm not old. You think that because you're a twerp. You're not a person yet.

CHARLIE gestures, hitting her on the head.

LEAH: Stand still.—You're only half-made.

CHARLIE: I'm grownup. I'm getting married.

LEAH: You're not old enough to get married. I'll bet you don't even have a peepee yet. You probably don't have a peepee yet.

RAINBOW: Don't let her talk to you like that, Charlie. I wouldn't let her talk to me like that.

CHARLIE: She's a crazy old witch. You think I listen to what she says?

NADINE: Show respect. Don't pay any attention to him, Leah. You can't teach kids respect nowadays. You think he listens to me? He don't. I tell him he should marry someone rich, but he don't. Look who he's getting married to.

LEAH looks at BIRDIE.

NADINE: Birdie!

CHARLIE: And why not?

NADINE: Look at her!

They look at BIRDIE. She continues sewing a moment. Then she looks at them.

BIRDIE: What?

NADINE: See what I mean?

CHARLIE: And where would I find someone rich?

NADINE: Have you looked?

CHARLIE: If I had the right clothes …

NADINE: With your looks?

CHARLIE: I need a good suit.

NADINE: You don't need a suit.

BIRDIE puts on the veil. It covers her face.

BIRDIE: How does it look?

NADINE: See that?

LEAH: Let's see, Birdie.

BIRDIE turns to LEAH.

NADINE: Is there something you can do about that veil, Leah?

BIRDIE turns to NADINE.

LEAH: Let's see.

BIRDIE turns to LEAH.

LEAH: I don't know, Nadine.

NADINE: *(Pointing to* BIRDIE.*)* Look at that … *(Pointing to* CHARLIE.*)* Then look at him.—A prince.

CHARLIE: *(As he takes his pants off.)* Thanks, Mom.

NADINE: He could've married money.

CHARLIE: You hear that, Birdie?

NADINE: Sure.

CHARLIE: Oh, Mom.

NADINE: Oh, Charlie.

BIRDIE looks up.

NADINE: Why are you wearing that lipstick?

BIRDIE: 'Cause I put it on. Okay?

NADINE turns up her eyes.

NADINE: You see, Leah?

CHARLIE: It's okay, Mom.

NADINE: Things were different when we were growing up, Leah. Weren't they?

LEAH: Yes they were.

NADINE: Did you ever get married, Leah?

LEAH: No, Nadine. Did you?

NADINE: Never. Once I did. *(Touching her heart.)* Here.

LEAH: Who was that?

NADINE: Charlie's dad. He got inside my heart. And I couldn't pull him out. Then little Charlie came, and I had to take care of him, so I couldn't work. I had to ask his dad if he'd take care of us. He said yes, but he didn't. The obligation. He'd go off and drink and stay away for days.—He got a woman.

LEAH: Did she give him money?

NADINE: Money?

LEAH: Did you?

NADINE: I never gave him money.

LEAH: You see him?

NADINE: Him?

LEAH: Yeah.

NADINE: In the street.

LEAH: Alone?

NADINE: Me?

LEAH: Is he alone?

NADINE: He is not alone. He's never alone.

LEAH: Was she pretty?

NADINE: She wasn't pretty.

LEAH: What did she look like?

NADINE: Like a dog. Worse. *(Pause.)* I had a baby.

LEAH: Rainbow.

NADINE: Before Rainbow. Ray. I was sick. I couldn't take care of him. I couldn't feed him. I thought I was going to die. I had no milk in my breasts. Charlie was older and could fend for himself. But not little Ray. I had to give him up.—They thought I was going to die, and I gave him up. He was cute. He had pretty eyes.—I don't know where he is. He's all right, though. He's with a family, like his own. They say he's all right. He goes to school.

RAINBOW sits on NADINE's lap..

NADINE: I should've given this one away, too.

RAINBOW: Oh, Mom.

NADINE: Life with me isn't good. It's no good for the kids. I have nothing good to give them, nothing to teach them. I'm a whore. That's what I have to do to feed them. *(There is a pause.)* Did you know that? At least the kids don't see what I do.

LEAH: They can hear you, Nadine.

NADINE: They don't see it. At least they don't see it. *(She rocks RAINBOW.)* It's hard on them.

RAINBOW and BIRDIE do a little veil dance.

Scene 3

BIRDIE sits at the table. She wears a sweater. She is finishing eating a sandwich. RAINBOW sits on the mattress. She has just eaten. There are two plates and silver on the table.

BIRDIE: My mother died of emphysema, couldn't breathe. They put tubes in her. Up her nose, up her private parts, up the veins in her arms. I wouldn't want any of that done to me. Even if I'm going to die. When I die, I'll just die. That stuff doesn't save you. It just makes you look ugly. I'd rather just die. The longer they keep you, the uglier you look.—I don't think I'm ever going to be fat. I'm too skinny.

RAINBOW: Hmm.

BIRDIE: In the home, there was a girl who was nice. She never said anything unless she meant it. And no one could make her say anything she didn't mean. She had no teeth, and she'd say to me, "Your problems are my problems." She meant that if I had a problem she'd help. And that was very nice, but all the kids laughed at her because she had no teeth and they didn't understand her when she talked. *(She eats.)* I never did any whoring either. Not me. I wouldn't do anything like that. I can't stand someone telling me what to do. And I couldn't stand someone touching me unless I wanted it. I don't care how much they'd pay. Charlie's always telling me to do this and to do that, because everybody bosses him. He thinks because we're married he should be bossing me. Nadine hates me and won't stop until she sees me out of here.

NADINE enters. She goes to the table, takes the silver from the table, goes to the sideboard, opens a drawer, gives a suspicious look to BIRDIE, counts the silver in the drawer, puts the silver in, closes the drawer, gives another suspicious look to BIRDIE, and exits.

BIRDIE: Did you see that?

RAINBOW: What?

BIRDIE: Your mother. She thinks I'm going to steal something. I don't like that, and I don't like being looked at weird either.

RAINBOW: I don't look at you weird.

BIRDIE: You don't, but she does. I'm getting out of here.

RAINBOW: Where are you going?

BIRDIE: I don't need a place.

RAINBOW: You don't?

BIRDIE: I can sleep in the street.

RAINBOW: Really?

BIRDIE: You can come with me if you want.

RAINBOW: And sleep in the street?

BIRDIE: Yeah.

RAINBOW: Nuh-uh.

BIRDIE: Well, I'm going even if you're not.

RAINBOW: You have money?

BIRDIE: No.

RAINBOW: You need money.

BIRDIE: What for?

RAINBOW: To eat.

BIRDIE: You call this eating here?

RAINBOW: It's better than nothing.

BIRDIE: It stinks.

RAINBOW: How about Charlie?

BIRDIE: He can leave, too, if he wants.—I was better off in the home. They didn't treat me like a criminal there. She's always watching me. She doesn't watch you! How many times is she going to count the silver? She thinks I'm going to steal her crummy forks. She's worse than the matrons in prison.

RAINBOW: In prison?

BIRDIE: Yeah, prison. No one there was as bad. Not even the torturer.

RAINBOW: Torturer?

BIRDIE: Sure. A big ugly torturer with a big ugly sore on her lip.

RAINBOW: Did she hurt you?

BIRDIE: Sure. Plenty. She twisted our fingers and toes till we thought they were going to fall off.

RAINBOW: What for?

BIRDIE: Are you kidding? To hurt us.

RAINBOW: What for?

BIRDIE: Are you kidding? To find out something, or to punish us for something. She liked to give us pain. Or else she tried to drown us.

RAINBOW: Drown you?

BIRDIE: Yeah. She'd put our head in the water and hold it there till we started to drown. Then she'd pull it up and say, "Ready to talk?" We couldn't talk because we had water coming out of our mouth and nose and ears. So she'd say, "Okay. If you don't want to talk, take this." And she'd push our head in the water again. Someone said that Kitty was a dyke, and that she liked hurting us because she knew we wouldn't go for her. She didn't have to ask, because she knew what the answer would be, "No, you pig." *(She laughs heartily.)* "No, you pig." That's what we'd say to her. *(She laughs.)* Some people said she had cancer on her lip, but no one gave a damn. That's how much nobody cared about her. Because she was so mean. We were not allowed to smoke, but I smoked. They would catch me by the smell in my mouth. She was a pervert. She liked to put her nose in my mouth. She was always calling me in to smell my mouth. One day I bit her nose. She was going to report me, but I paid her off.

RAINBOW: You paid her?

BIRDIE: I had money. I worked at the shop. We made shoes. I liked to work to keep my mind off how unhappy I was.

CHARLIE enters with LUCILLE. He sits in the rocking chair, rocks her to sleep, and hums.

BIRDIE: He's always telling me what to do because everyone tells him what to do.

CHARLIE: Who tells me what to do?

PETE enters left and hides behind the tree.

BIRDIE: Everyone tells you what to do. Nadine tells you what to do and Pete tells you what to do. So you think that getting married means that you get to boss me. But no one tells me what to do— *(To RAINBOW.)* He says he's the boss. But look at him, he's skin and bones. You see this sweater? It's too small for me. Well, I'm going to give it to Charlie, because he's skinnier than me. He gets angry, but that's a reality. Charlie said we're going to be on our own. But now he says he can't leave Lucille. Well, he cares more about Lucille and Nadine and the whole lot of them than he cares for me. *(Standing.)* I want something from life. Do something. *(She starts to walk left. She sees PETE.)* What's he doing? He's always staring at me! He just stands there and stares at me! You Peeping Tom!

RAINBOW: Who's that?

BIRDIE: Pete.

CHARLIE: What are you looking at? Fuckhead!

CHARLIE goes towards the tree. LUCILLE starts to cry.

CHARLIE: Yeah, you! Fuckhead! Yeah! Fuckhead! You! Yeah, you! Fuckhead! *(He returns to the rocking chair.)* Fuckhead! *(He rocks LUCILLE. To himself.)* Fuckhead.

PETE: *(Shouting from behind the tree.)* I'm sick and tired of the whole lot of you!

CHARLIE: Shut your trap! I'm trying to put Lucille to sleep!

PETE: Always trying to get something for nothing! You hoodlums! Well, forget it! My money is mine, and I'm keeping it! You won't get nothing for nothing! You hear that? Mine! You hear that? It's my money! And I get to keep it! And if you want it, you're gonna have to send the pretty girl to get it! Come and get it, Birdie! I have a birdie inside my pants waiting for you!

CHARLIE: *(Starting to stand.)* You scum.—

PETE: Come here, girlie, tweet tweet!

CHARLIE: You take that back! *(Holding LUCILLE on the left arm and throwing punches with his right.)* Come out and fight!—Rainbow!!

RAINBOW runs to CHARLIE's side.

CHARLIE: Take Lucille!

RAINBOW *takes* LUCILLE *and exits right.*

CHARLIE: I'm going to tear you to pieces, Pete!

PETE: Come on, Charlie! I always wanted to hear your tiny bones cracking! Crackle crackle! Come on!

CHARLIE: *(Shadowboxing.)* Come out, you yellow-bellied scum!

PETE: Take one more step and I'm gonna make you swallow your teeth.

CHARLIE: You're a coward, Pete!

PETE: Yeah? Say goodbye, Charlie. Say goodbye.

BIRDIE: Why don't you get yourself a date so you don't have to stand behind trees touching yourself?

PETE: Come a little closer, you little slut! And I'll show you what I can put inside you!

CHARLIE: You bloodsucker! That's my wife you're talking to! I'm going to push your face through your head! Come out! You coward! I'm not going to work for you anymore!

PETE: Who're you going to work for, peewee?

CHARLIE: *(Getting closer to the tree as* PETE *moves left.)* Don't make me lose my temper. Fuckhead.

PETE: Sure.

CHARLIE: *(Reaching the tree as* PETE *moves further left.)* Scram!

PETE *shadowboxes as he moves towards the tree.* CHARLIE *shadowboxes as he retreats. They freeze for a moment, then* CHARLIE *mumbles some words and sits in the rocking chair.*

PETE: Yeah! You stay there, boy. And don't come too close to me, or I may hit you hard. And don't ask me to feel sorry for you, because I've had it with feeling sorry for you. I'm sick, and nobody feels sorry for me. I'm going to die in the gutter, and nobody's going to feel sorry for me or come ask me if I need anything. The dogs will see me dead, and they'll just come eat me like dead meat. People eat animal dead meat, and animals eat human dead meat if they can. They can tell you're dead because you get cold, and also because you don't move when they get close to you and nudge you, or when they growl at you, or when they start digging their teeth into you.

I'm saving money to buy me a cemetery lot so I don't have to lay in the street till the garbage collector comes to get me. I'm getting my corner in the cemetery, and I'm getting myself buried when I die so no one can mess with me.

BIRDIE: Goodbye, Charlie. I'm leaving now.

CHARLIE: Don't go, Birdie.

BIRDIE: You'll never leave, Charlie.

CHARLIE: I will, Birdie, I will.

BIRDIE: You'll never leave Lucille.

CHARLIE: I will.

BIRDIE: And you'll never leave Rainbow.

CHARLIE: I will.

BIRDIE: You'll never leave.

CHARLIE: I will, Birdie.

BIRDIE: Come now! Leave with me now!

CHARLIE: I can't!

RAINBOW: Get up and leave with me now!

CHARLIE: I can't now, Birdie. How can I?

BIRDIE: You'll never leave.

CHARLIE: Birdie. I'm tied down. I have to help Nadine. I gotta. I can't leave.

BIRDIE: Oh! Charlie! *(She starts to go.)* Goodbye!

CHARLIE: Try to understand, Birdie. *(Going on his knees.)* I beg you, Birdie. Things will work out. You want to see me down? *(Going flat on the floor.)* My face is on the floor, Birdie. You want to see dirt on my face? *(He rubs his face on the floor.)* Here's dirt on my face. Birdie. Don't leave. Don't go, Birdie, I can't stand it if you leave. Birdie.

BIRDIE exits. RAINBOW enters. She is wrapped in a blanket. CHARLIE mumbles and cries and sobs, his face still on the floor.

RAINBOW: *(Softly.)* Birdie ... don't leave.

PETE *comes out from behind the tree. He raises his hands after* BIRDIE *questioningly.*

PETE: Birdie … ?

Springtime

CHARACTERS

RAINBOW: Twenty-nine years old. Slim and spirited.
GRETA: Twenty-six years old. Slim, handsome, and shy.
RAY: Twenty-seven years old. High-strung and handsome. He wears a dark suit.

In a small Eastern city. 1958.

Scene 1: *Greta is ill*

RAINBOW's bedroom. A small room. On the left wall, upstage, there is a small door; downstage of the door there is a small window. Downstage of the window there is a chair. In the up righthand corner of the room there is a small bed with metal foot- and headboard. On the bed there is a nightgown. To the left of the bed there is a night table. On the night table there is a book, a pitcher of water, and a glass. On the back wall there hangs a painting of a landscape. RAINBOW and GRETA have just entered. GRETA takes off her dress, sits on the bed, and starts to put on the nightgown.

RAINBOW: Don't worry, Greta. I know what to do.

GRETA: What, Rainbow? What can you do?

RAINBOW: I'll find some money. Don't worry.

GRETA: How?

RAINBOW: I'll find money, Greta. I can't tell you how.

GRETA: Why not?

RAINBOW: You won't love me anymore if I tell you how.

GRETA: Tell me.

RAINBOW: Please don't make me tell you.

GRETA: I don't want you to do anything that would make you ashamed.

RAINBOW: I've been in jail.

GRETA: Why? What did you do?

RAINBOW helps GRETA lie down. She covers her with the sheet.

GRETA: Tell me.

RAINBOW: I've been in jail for stealing.

GRETA: Stealing?

RAINBOW: Yes. I haven't done it since I've known you. But now I must do it again. You're ill and we must take care of you.

GRETA: No! I don't want you to steal for me. You'll be arrested. You'll go to jail. You mustn't.

RAINBOW: I must, my darling.

There is a silence. GRETA *puts her face on the pillow and sobs.*

Scene 2: *Stealing for Greta*

GRETA *is lying in bed.* RAINBOW *sits on the chair.*

RAINBOW: I got it off his pocket. He came out of the store and put it in his pocket. I grabbed it and ran. He ran after me and grabbed me. He tripped. I yanked my arm off and I threw him. Look. He tore my sleeve. *(Putting a wristwatch in* GRETA's *hand.)* He ran after me, but I was gone. Went in a building and hid. Saw him pass. Went to the back of the building and got out through the yard. I was afraid to go into the street. I was afraid he might have gone around the block. There was no one there. I walked to the corner and grabbed a bus. I didn't look like a thief. Would anyone think I'm a thief? Wasn't out of breath. Sat calmly— *(Getting the watch from* GRETA.*)* It's a good watch.

GRETA: Get rid of it.

RAINBOW: I'll sell it.

GRETA: To whom?

RAINBOW: I'll find a buyer.

GRETA: I'm afraid.

RAINBOW: Don't be.

GRETA: Just get rid of it.

RAINBOW: We need the money. For you. To make you well.

Scene 3: *Rainbow is caught*

RAINBOW's hand covers her cheek. She has turned away from GRETA. GRETA lies on the bed.

GRETA: Look at me! Who hurt you like that?

RAINBOW turns to face GRETA.

GRETA: Who did that to you?

RAINBOW: The man whose watch I took.

GRETA: I knew you'd get hurt. I knew you couldn't do what you were doing and not get hurt.

RAINBOW: I got careless. I went back to where I got the watch.

GRETA: Why?

RAINBOW: He came from behind. He grabbed me and made me go with him.

GRETA: Where?

RAINBOW: To his place.

GRETA: Oh!

RAINBOW: I tried to get away. He forced me. I resisted, and he pushed me in. He said he'd put me in jail.

GRETA: What did he do to you!

RAINBOW: I had to agree.

GRETA: To what?

RAINBOW: To do something for him.

GRETA: What!

RAINBOW: Meet someone.

GRETA: Who!

RAINBOW: He didn't say.

GRETA: What for?

RAINBOW: He's nasty.

GRETA: Are you afraid?

RAINBOW: Yes.

Scene 4: *Greta wonders if Rainbow loves Ray*

GRETA *lies in bed.* RAINBOW *stands left.*

RAINBOW: He's like a snake.

GRETA: Do you love him?

RAINBOW: Love him? I hate him. He hates me. He hates me for no reason. Not because of the watch. He never cared about the watch. Just for no reason. He never cared about the watch. That was nothing for him. He hates me. Just because he wants to.—I hate him, but I have a reason. *(She goes to the chair.)* I understand him, though.

GRETA: You do?

RAINBOW: Yes.

GRETA: How can you?

RAINBOW: I think in his heart of hearts he's not the way he appears to be.

GRETA: What is he like? He couldn't be good and do what he does.

RAINBOW: Well, he's not what he appears to be.

Pause.

GRETA: … Could I have some water?

RAINBOW *pours water. She lifts* GRETA's *head up and holds the glass to* GRETA's *lips. When* GRETA *drinks,* RAINBOW *puts the glass down and sits.*

GRETA: Didn't you already do what you had to do for him? Didn't you already pay—for the watch? Why do you still have to work for him?

RAINBOW: He's a friend.

GRETA: If I die … Will you love him then?

RAINBOW: … If you die?— *(She goes to the side of the bed and kneels.)* If you die, I'll love you—whether you live or die, it's you I love. And if I ever love anyone else, it won't be Ray. Not Ray. Never Ray.

GRETA *laughs.*

Scene 5: *Heute sind Kleider eng*

RAINBOW sweeps the floor.

GRETA: You never wear clothes that fit.

RAINBOW: This?

GRETA: That's a size too small.

RAINBOW: It's my size.

GRETA: Clothes should be looser.

RAINBOW: Not any more, madam. Now clothes are tight—how do you say that in German?

GRETA: What?

RAINBOW: What I just said.

GRETA: What?

RAINBOW: Now clothes are tight.

GRETA: *Heute sind Kleider eng.*

RAINBOW: *(Mispronouncing.) Heute sind Kleider eng.*

GRETA: *(Impatiently.) Heute sind Kleider eng.*

RAINBOW: How do you say, "You lose your temper too easily?"

GRETA: Who?

RAINBOW: You.

GRETA: I lose my temper?

RAINBOW: Yes.

GRETA: I don't.

RAINBOW: How do you say it?

GRETA: That I lose my temper?

RAINBOW: Yes.

GRETA: I don't lose my temper.

RAINBOW: How do you say it?

GRETA: *Ich werde niemals heftig.*

RAINBOW: *Ich werde niemals heftig* ... I love German. *(She swoons to the floor.)* ... I love German.

GRETA: That means, "I don't lose my temper." Ha!

Scene 6: *Ray gives advice to Rainbow*

RAINBOW stands right, fluffing the pillow. GRETA sits up against the headboard.

RAINBOW: Can you imagine?—And I said to him, "It's you who places too much importance on whether I like men or I like women. For me it's not important. What's important is that, since I met Greta, it's only she I love." *(Placing the pillow behind GRETA.)* "That's what's important." *(Taking the bedspread off the bed.)* "Why should it be important whether I like men or women? Does it make any difference to anyone?"— *(Taking the bedspread out the door to shake it.)* "If it doesn't make any difference to anyone, why should anyone care?" *(Turning to GRETA.)* He said, "If it doesn't make any difference, why don't you choose to love a man?" And I said, "It doesn't make a difference to anyone else, but of course, it makes a difference to me." *(Placing the cover over GRETA.)* If I don't like men, why should I pretend that I do? Why should I try to love someone I don't love when I already love someone I love? And besides, do you think it makes a difference to anyone?

GRETA: I suppose it doesn't make any difference to anyone.

RAINBOW: That's right. Why should I force myself. *(Sitting next to GRETA.)* And he said, "What difference does anything make? Live, die, it doesn't make any difference." And I said, "Live or die makes a difference. I want to live, and I want to be happy, but I don't care about the things you care about." And he said, "What things?" And I said, *(Walking to the chair.)* "The way you see things." And I said that I'm not going to pretend to see life the way he does. And he said, "Why not?" that he thought I should. And he said that I should care about those things, and if I don't, I should pretend that I do. And I said, *(Sitting.)* "Why?" And he said that he talks to me as a brother would, for my own good. And I said I thought he had some nerve, because I thought his life was far from impeccable—far from it.—And I told him that.

GRETA: His life is far from impeccable.

RAINBOW: I told him he had some nerve.

GRETA: Your life is impeccable now.—I don't see anything wrong with it.

RAINBOW: ... Neither do I.

GRETA: Your life was peccable when you were working for him. But now that you've paid your debt to him, and you don't work for him anymore, your life is impeccable. It was he who made your life peccable.

RAINBOW *laughs.*

GRETA: Why do you laugh?

RAINBOW: How do you say peccable in German?

GRETA: Why?

Scene 7: *Greta wonders how Rainbow sees things*

GRETA *lies in bed.* RAINBOW *sits by the window looking out into the yard.*

RAINBOW: With time and money, they look better and better.

GRETA: What, honey?

RAINBOW: The flowers.

GRETA: How could that be?

RAINBOW: Maybe it's the fertilizer I put in the soil.

GRETA: What looks better?

RAINBOW: The colors. They look healthier.

GRETA: How do you see things? Do you see things different from the way I see them?

RAINBOW: Why do you ask?

GRETA: *(Smiling.)* ... I just wondered.

RAINBOW: Why?

GRETA: I was worried ...

RAINBOW: That we see things differently ... ?

GRETA: Yes.

RAINBOW: We don't.

Scene 8: *Greta discovers what Rainbow does for Ray*

GRETA *is standing on the chair. She is opening an envelope. She takes out some pictures and looks through them with alarm. She throws them on the floor and stares into space. RAINBOW enters. She looks at the pictures on the floor. Then she looks at GRETA.*

GRETA: Is that what you do for him?

RAINBOW *kneels down to get the pictures. GRETA tries to reach for the pictures.*

GRETA: Why! Why!

GRETA *starts pounding on RAINBOW. RAINBOW tries to hold her down.*

GRETA: Why! Why are you doing that when I asked you not to? Why do you do that?—Why do you do that?—Why do you do that?! You're lying naked with that man! Who is that man? What is he doing to you? Why do you do that?! Why do you take your clothes off?! Why do you take such pictures?!

RAINBOW: I'm sorry! I'm sorry!

GRETA: Why do you do that!

RAINBOW: I have to.

GRETA: Why!

RAINBOW: Because you must have treatment.

GRETA *cries.*

RAINBOW: I don't mind. It's for you.

GRETA *sobs.*

RAINBOW: It's for you.

Scene 9: *Greta admires the sunlight*

The shutter is closed. GRETA sits upstage of the window. The chair faces front. RAINBOW stands next to her.

GRETA: Could you open the window?

RAINBOW *opens the window.*

GRETA: I like to sit here and see the sun coming in. I like to let it come in through the open window. The sun is brighter that way—or so it seems to me. There are times when I feel disturbed. I feel restless. I feel nasty. And looking at the sun coming in makes me feel calm.

Scene 10: *Greta thinks that Ray is in love*

GRETA stands left of the bed straightening the bed. RAINBOW sits in the chair.

GRETA: Ray was here this afternoon.

RAINBOW: What did he want?

GRETA: He didn't say.—He waited for you and then he left.— *(She starts moving down as she straightens the side of the bed.)* Does he sound to you like he's in love?

RAINBOW: No.

GRETA: He sounds to me like he's in love.

RAINBOW: Who with?

GRETA: I don't know, but he sounds to me like he's in love.

RAINBOW: How does a person in love sound?

GRETA sits on the right side of the bed.

GRETA: A person in love holds his breath a little after inhaling or while they inhale. They inhale, stop for a moment, and inhale a little more.

RAINBOW: I haven't seen him do that. *(She lies on the bed.)*

GRETA: I have.

RAINBOW: He seems preoccupied to me.

GRETA: Yes, I think he sounds preoccupied. Maybe he's lost money on the market.

RAINBOW: Maybe he has. Why are you concerned about him?

GRETA: I'm not.

RAINBOW: You sound concerned.

GRETA: He's preoccupied.

Scene 11: *Rainbow doesn't feel loved anymore*

Greta lies in bed. Rainbow stands by the door facing her.

RAINBOW: Something's wrong. Something's wrong, because you're not happy, because you have to keep things from me. I know you don't tell me what you think—not everything. Did you ever keep things from me before? Is this something new, or have you always kept things from me? *(Pause.)* Is it that you don't love me anymore?

GRETA: *(Shaking her head.)* No.

RAINBOW: For me to love is to adore. And to be loved is to be adored. So I never felt I was loved before. Till I met you. But I don't feel loved anymore.

Scene 12: *Ray wants something from Greta*

Greta lies in bed. Ray stands to the left of the bed by her feet, facing her. She is frightened like a trapped cat.

GRETA: I lash out at you because I can't deal with you. I can't even understand what you are.

In the course of the speech, Ray moves closer and closer to her and starts to lean towards her. She recoils.

GRETA: You're like some kind of animal who comes to me with strange problems, to make strange demands on me.

Greta pushes Ray off. He persists.

GRETA: You come in all sweaty and hungry, and you say you want this and you want that. Take your hands away from me! Not again! Not again! Never again! Don't touch me! Leave me be! I have nothing to give you. Don't tell me that you want these things. Talk about something else. What else can you talk about?

Rainbow enters. She is obviously alarmed. She looks at Greta, then at Ray; then at Greta again. Greta turns her head away and sobs. Rainbow and Ray look at each other.

Scene 13: *Rainbow leaves Greta*

Rainbow stands at the door looking out. Greta sits on the bed looking at her.

"Melancholy Baby" is heard:

> "Come to me, my melancholy baby.
> Just cuddle up and don't be blue.
> All your fears are foolish fancy, baby.
> You know, honey, I'm in love with you."

GRETA *moves to the chair. She sits facing* RAINBOW. *She looks down.*

> "Every cloud must have a silver lining."

GRETA *looks at* RAINBOW.

> "So wait until the sun shines through.
> Smile, my honey, dear,
> While I kiss away each tear.
> Or else I shall be melancholy too."

GRETA *reaches out and takes* RAINBOW's *hand.* RAINBOW *allows* GRETA *to hold her hand, but does not respond.*

> "Come sweetheart mine
> Don't sit and pine.
> Tell me all the cares
> That made you feel so blue.
> I'm sorry, hon."

RAINBOW *faces* GRETA.

> "What have I done.
> Have I ever said
> An unkind word to you.
> My love is true."

RAINBOW *leans over and puts her head next to* GRETA's.

> "And just for you.
> I'll do almost anything
> At any time.
> Hear when you sigh
> Or when you cry.
> Something seems to grieve
> This very heart of mine.
> Come to me my melancholy baby.
> Just cuddle up and don't be blue."

RAINBOW *walks to the door and stands there looking out for a while. Then she exits while the song plays to the end.* GRETA *lowers her head. Then she looks to the back. As the song is coming to an end, she looks down again.*

Scene 14: *Greta reads Rainbow's letter*

GRETA *walks to the chair holding a book. She sits down and opens the book. An envelope falls from it. She opens the envelope, takes out a letter, and reads it.*

GRETA: "My beloved,—I'm sometimes obliged to do things that are dangerous,—and to do things that I hate. To befriend people and then betray them. Someday I may be hurt. If this happens, and I'm not able to tell you this, I hope one day you'll open this book and find this note. I love you more than anything in the world, and it is to you that I owe my happiness. I always felt that I didn't want to love only halfway, that I wanted to love with all my heart or not at all, and that I wanted to be loved the same way or not at all. With you, I had this, and if anything happens to me, I wanted you to remember this: that you are my angel, and I will always love you. Even after death. Forever yours,—Rainbow."

Lust

CHARACTERS

RAY: Thirty-seven to fifty-two years old. Passionate and driven.
JOSEPH: Fifty-five to seventy years old. A self-contained businessman.
HELENA: Twenty-five to forty years old. A beautiful and sensitive upper-class
woman.
JIM: A car mechanic.
SHE: A woman with a loud mouth.
LORRAINE: A woman in a housedress.
WANG: A Chinese man in traditional embroidered clothes.
GIRL: A girl in Victorian clothes.
WING: A Chinese woman in traditional embroidered clothes.
BOY: A boy in black satin Chinese clothes and cap.
BIRDIE: Forty-nine years old. Subdued, honest, and well-meaning.

In a major city. 1968 to 1983.

SCENES 1–5:

*On the right side of the stage is RAY and HELENA's bedroom; on the left is JOSEPH's
office. The two rooms are divided by a couch that faces left and two easy chairs
that face right. The furniture suggests a futuristic or art deco style. Behind the
back wall there is a platform that runs the width of the stage.*

*The bedroom. On the back wall of the bedroom there is a door. On the up right
side there is a bed with a satin cover. There is a straight chair to the left of the bed
and two easy chairs on the left facing right.*

*The office. On the back wall of the office there is a door. In the up left corner there
is a desk. On the upstage side of the desk there is a chair facing front. There is
another chair against the right side of the desk facing front, and another against
the left wall facing right.*

SCENE 6: THE DREAM.

The back wall of the set is removed, exposing the platform.

   a. The car repair shop. This is played on the right side of the platform.

   *b. A bathroom door in a working-class apartment. On the left of the platform
there is a door with a full-length mirror.*

   c. A fire escape. A scaffolding against the left wall. There is a milk crate on it.

   *d. A Chinese restaurant. On the down side of the platform, between the steps,
there is the window of a Chinese restaurant. A sheet of plastic is stretched*

over it. There is a small wooden box on each side of the window. On the stage floor, up center, there is a dining table. On the down side of the table there is a chair that faces up.

e. The restaurant basement. This is performed down-center stage.

f. The streets of Bolivia. This is performed on the platform.

SCENES 7–11:

The stage is restored to its original setting.

Scene 1

In JOSEPH's office. There is a blanket on the down side of the sofa. JOSEPH stands to the left of the desk.

RAY: The boy's eleven. He has difficulty at school. He can't concentrate. He gets distracted, and he has a problem with discipline. Not discipline in the sense that he's unruly. He's well-behaved. *(He sits on the sofa.)* But he doesn't do his work well. He's fallen behind, and he keeps falling behind. He's small for his age, and he's thin and underdeveloped.

JOSEPH: Why are you telling me this?

RAY: Because I want you to help him. He's been expelled from school. His parents are very poor. The kid's undernourished. He should stay in a boys' residence. He's bright. He'll do well if he gets financial help.

While RAY speaks, JOSEPH sits next to him. He reaches for the blanket and covers their middles. He puts his arm around RAY's waist and twists him around so RAY's back is to him. He pulls RAY's pants down and begins to move his pelvis against him.

RAY: He needs nourishment and physical therapy. I'm asking the foundation to help him financially. Can the foundation pay his tuition at a boarding school that can handle learning problems, to give him that chance, perhaps to save his life?

JOSEPH: How can I help?

RAY: With a scholarship and additional funds for medical expenses.—Is this ordinary, is this the way you conduct business?

JOSEPH: Yes, frequently. This is frequently the way I conduct business. It doesn't interfere with business. Yes, we can continue our discussion as we do this.

RAY: I may not be able to speak clearly as you do what you're doing.

JOSEPH: I would prefer not to stop now.

RAY: No,—I'm not asking you to stop.

JOSEPH: Yes. What should I do for the boy?

RAY: He needs help.

JOSEPH: What kind of help?

They both climax.

JOSEPH: How old is he?

RAY: Eight.

JOSEPH: Put in a request to the foundation. I'll advise them in his favor. I'm sure it's a good investment.

JOSEPH zips himself up and stands up. RAY adjusts his pants and removes the blanket.

RAY: By the way, I enjoyed that very much.

JOSEPH: I did, too. Anytime you feel up to it again, give me a ring. I thought it was quite pleasant. Very natural.

RAY: I thought so, too.

HELENA: *(In a low voice from offstage.)* ... Father.

JOSEPH: Come in, Helena.

HELENA enters.

HELENA: I didn't mean to interrupt. It's two, and you had asked me to come at two. Would you prefer it if I came back later?

JOSEPH: No, Ray and I are finished. Do you know each other?

HELENA: Yes, Father.

RAY: How are you, Helena?

HELENA: I'm very well, Ray. I am so glad to see you. *(She sits behind the desk.)* Ray has a savage nature, Father. Have you found this out about him yet?

JOSEPH: ... No.

RAY: I never thought I did.

HELENA: You do.

RAY: How?

HELENA: You're wild, Ray.

RAY: How?

HELENA: You're wild like earth full of worms. Worms that shout.—If you can imagine that. And so are you, Father. You're also wild. I'm not. My earth doesn't have living creatures in it. I am like milk. I have milk in my veins. That's perfectly all right. I don't mean that I'm dead or anything like that. Milk is a good substance. I am clear and liquid and fine. I enjoy your being the way you are. It amuses me and delights me. There is something dear about your wildness. *(She falls to the floor. She remains still for a moment.)* It's a bitter thing.

RAY kneels next to her and helps her up.

JOSEPH: Are you all right?

HELENA: *(To JOSEPH.)* Yes, Father. I love you. I have always loved you. Even if I've never been close to you. I tell you this now, so strangely like this, because I feel a strange urgency to tell you that I love you. That you are the person who has enriched my life, and that I feel grateful to you and will be grateful to you as long as I live. I'm sorry to behave this way. I know I'm acting very strangely. Perhaps it's because I'm going to die. Perhaps I'm going crazy.—I'm going up now. Don't worry about me. I am happy and I'm very well. Even if I sound as if I am perfectly insane.

She starts to move. JOSEPH stops her and kisses her on the cheek. His movements are clumsy. She exits. JOSEPH and RAY look at each other.

RAY: Do you think she's all right?

Pause.

JOSEPH: Would you marry Helena, Ray?

RAY thinks a moment.

RAY: Yes.

JOSEPH: Thank you.

RAY looks at JOSEPH for a moment; then he looks away.

Scene 2

In RAY *and* HELENA'S *bedroom.* HELENA *is lying in bed under the covers.* RAY *sits on the chair to the left of the bed. His jacket and necktie are off. They hold hands as they speak. They both look front.*

RAY: I was two or three. I remember some things. My parents, my adoptive parents, came to the agency and took me to their home. They were kind, but I felt very strange and isolated at first. They were dutiful, honest, and gentle, and they provided for my needs. Modestly. But I never lacked anything material or emotional. What I got from them would have sufficed, but I'd come to them with a fever, a fever placed in my heart by my mother. A fever that has never left me.

HELENA: An illness?

RAY: … A hunger.

HELENA: For food?

RAY: … Yes … For food.

HELENA: How I wish I knew what I hunger for.

RAY: I remember her voice. Husky. I remember her arms. Being in her arms. And I remember the fever we all shared … The hunger.

HELENA: Who were the others?

RAY: My brother, my sister.

HELENA: Have you ever tried to find them?

RAY: No.

HELENA: Why not?

Ray is absorbed in his thoughts.

RAY: I never have. *(Pause.)* Never have …

HELENA: Do you love your adoptive parents?

RAY: I do. Yes, I do. *(There is a pause.)* But can you ever forget the arms that first held you?

HELENA: … No.

RAY: Your mother's?

HELENA: She never really held me. Hardly ever.

RAY: Who did?

HELENA: I remember the arms that didn't hold me. *(Pause.)* Come to bed.

RAY is thinking of something else. HELENA looks at him. She lets go of his hand, turns from him, and curls up on her side of the bed.

Scene 3

In JOSEPH's office. RAY sits on the chair to the right of the desk. JOSEPH stands in the up right corner.

RAY: The human being is sinister. It's morbid. It's morbid. It's morbid. It's perverse. It's serving a devil.

JOSEPH: Why do you say that?

RAY: It's serving another species. Is there a species that controls us? That seeks revenge upon us?—A species that aims to destroy us? Are we doing this ourselves? Are we suicidal? Are we aiming to destroy ourselves?

JOSEPH: Why do you say that?

RAY: Don't you think we're destroying ourselves? We live in the future. We're robots. Have you realized that? Who thinks of the present? Our present is no use to us. Our present is a thing of the past. Our past is no use to us either. We have no reason to remember. If we think of something new, God loves us. It's an addiction. A daily dose. What's new? What's new? What's new? What's new? What's next? What's next?

JOSEPH: Ray. How long since you've had a vacation? A holiday.

Pause.

RAY: It's been some time.

JOSEPH: You should take one. *(He walks left and looks out.)* I make myself do it. Twice a year. Last time I went to Paris. I forced myself to stay. And I tried not to do too much. I hardly did any business. I did what other people do. I looked around. I saw some earrings that I wish I had bought for Helena. She would've looked good wearing them. She's elegant, like her mother. She is well made. Like a horse or a piece of art. You look at her from a distance, and you know it took time and craft and breeding to make her. There is something wrong with her, though, and I don't know what it is. But I don't understand women. I've never understood them. They're a different species. Don't you think, Ray? But I know there's something further wrong with her beyond what is wrong with women.—This business with technology. What do you have against it?

RAY: It will destroy us, Joseph. Can't you see that?

JOSEPH: Why don't you and Helena go away on a holiday?

Scene 4

In RAY and HELENA's bedroom. RAY is sitting in the downstage easy chair. HELENA is standing on the right side of the bed. She wears a slip and is putting on a dress. She continues dressing through the rest of the scene.

RAY: I see people drunk, unclean, unshaven, their clothes torn, their foul smell polluting the air. They don't know enough to wash. Mindless. Toothless. Their eyes in a daze. And I wonder, "When do you ever see an animal like that?" If they're physically ill. If they can't find food and they're undernourished and ill, perhaps. But no animal would ever be passive if there is food within their reach. No animal would leave a stone unturned if their health or survival is at stake. Humans don't learn much in a lifetime. They unlearn what has been learned by others.

HELENA: Humans can't find food under stones. Humans can't just sniff and find food. That's ridiculous. Food is many steps removed from man's reach.

RAY: You can figure out how to find it.

HELENA: It's harder for some.

RAY: Why is it harder?

HELENA: For some people it's not so easy. It's not so clear. *(Under breath.)* For some people, survival is not so clear.

RAY: How can anyone live and grow in such a state where survival is not clear?

HELENA: I would be at a loss if I had to earn my own living—

RAY: Oh, Helena, you. Of course you would.

HELENA: —if I couldn't depend on someone else's earning ability. *(Pause.)* I was talking to you. I was telling you something, and you never answered.

RAY: What were you saying?

HELENA: You never heard me?

RAY: I did, but I don't remember.

HELENA: I said I didn't like the play.

RAY: You didn't?

HELENA: No.

RAY: That's odd.

HELENA: Why odd?

RAY: I liked it.

HELENA: I didn't like the words.

RAY: What words?

HELENA: The words the author used.

RAY: The writing, you mean.

HELENA: I guess the writing. Some words in particular.

RAY: Which words?

HELENA: Words that are not real words. Like "likewise." False words that have nothing behind them.

RAY: Those are words that help get a thought through.

HELENA: No thinking goes into words like that.

RAY: New times need new words.

HELENA: Maybe so, for practical uses. But a lot of these words are a hoax. People feel good using them, but they feel a little cheated later, debilitated. If you speak without meaning, you feel debilitated.

Scene 5

In JOSEPH's *office.* RAY *enters holding a briefcase. He is walking hurriedly.* HELENA *is right behind him.* HELENA *stands upstage of the desk. She wears a jacket and hat. She carries a purse.*

HELENA: I asked you a question, and you didn't say anything.

RAY stands upstage of the chair and opens the briefcase. HELENA stands to his right.

RAY: I didn't.

HELENA: Why not?

RAY: *(Looking through papers in the briefcase.)* Because.

HELENA: Don't because me. I'm talking to you!

RAY: *(Slamming shut the briefcase and walking around the left of the desk to down right.)* What do you want?

HELENA: I asked you a question.

RAY: What was it?

HELENA: You didn't hear me?

RAY: *(Turning to her.)* No, I didn't.

HELENA: Why not?

RAY: I was thinking about something else.

HELENA: What were you thinking about?

RAY: *(Turning to her.)* Work! That's what I was thinking about! That's what I'm always thinking about. Work! *(Walking around the desk to her.)* That's all I think about. *(Through the following speech he grabs her by the wrist and twists her arm gradually.)* I don't need you for anything whatsoever—I go home to you each day. But I could go to an empty apartment as well—I go home to think about my work. About what I did during the day. What I did in the last ten years and what I'm going to do in the next ten years—I don't pretend to be thinking about anything else. I never did. I've never lied to you. I never said I would be thinking about anything else. I've never said, "I love you." I said, "The only thing I care about is my work." You never believed me when I told you. But I did tell you. Stop insisting, Helena. I don't hear you. You are like an insect smashing itself against my windshield. I don't hear you. And I don't see you! And I don't want to hear you! Or see you!

RAY pushes HELENA into the chair. HELENA lowers her head. She is desolate.

HELENA: What are you doing?

RAY: You're submissive!

HELENA: *(Reaching to him.)* … What do you mean? … Why do you say that? … What have I done?

He grabs and pushes her to the floor behind the desk. He starts crawling on all fours around the right of the desk towards the couch.

RAY: "What do you mean? Why do you say that?" Why don't you say something? Your eyes shift! You fret, but you say nothing! Why does it make you uncomfortable to hear me speak? Why is it hard for you to breathe?

HELENA: *(As she reaches the couch, she climbs on it and sits.)* Because I don't know what you mean or how to talk about it. I don't understand what you mean. I don't know what you're saying.—What do you mean? How does one talk about such things? I can't even understand what you're saying. It makes me very unhappy. I feel very unhappy.—I live in a fog, and I can't even talk about it. I don't know how to talk about it.—Do you? Can you talk about it? Can you help me?

Pause.

RAY: … I can't help you.

JOSEPH enters. He takes a couple of steps in. He looks at HELENA.

RAY: Animals are beautiful and refined and delicate. They are poised and elegant and intelligent. All their senses are put to use. They are delicate when they need to be and fierce when they need to be. They know how to obtain sustenance and shelter. They not only exercise when they need to chase after prey or get away from an animal that gives them chase, but they know when they need exercise, and run and play for no other reason than to keep in shape. *(Turning to JOSEPH.)* Haven't you seen animals playing in the fields? *(He looks at HELENA again.)* Human beings disintegrate morally unless they are under someone's constant surveillance. They need to be under constant commands, praise, penalties, abuse, rewards. They are slaves. There's nothing in them that lets them know if they're straying. They don't know if what they do is something that will destroy them. So they become slaves to whatever will take command of them,—instead of being guardians of their own selves. *(Pause.)* How can anyone be so unworthy of her own life?

HELENA weeps. JOSEPH goes to her. The lights go to black.

Scene 6

The following occurs simultaneously: Upbeat music is heard; color lights whirl all over the stage; the back wall of the set is removed; and the furniture is moved to the left and right, creating a clearing in the center. A projection on the rear wall reads: "Ray has a dream." WANG walks across to up center, then down center. His appearance and behavior mimic a traditional Chinese prototype.

WANG: Ray has a dream. *(He walks up, then left, and exits.)*

Dream a: A projection reads: "In a car repair shop." There is a piece of wood on the floor. RAY is waiting left. He feels his crotch. He shakes his leg. He feels his crotch again. JIM enters from the right. When he sees RAY, he becomes cautious. RAY turns to him. JIM picks up the piece of wood and holds it up in position to attack.

RAY: Easy …

JIM tightens up.

RAY: I'm just waiting for someone.

JIM: Who're you waiting for?

RAY: My girlfriend. She's working across the street.

JIM: And what's she doing there?

RAY: She's rehearsing. She'll be here in a few minutes.

JIM: What's she? A dancer?

RAY: An actress.

JIM: Really?

RAY: Yeah.

JIM: Is she in the movies?

RAY: She was in one.

JIM: You're pulling my leg.

RAY: I'm not.

JIM: *(Walking closer to RAY.)* And she's coming here?

RAY: Yeah.

JIM: I'll be damned.

JIM looks front. RAY looks at him.

RAY: I'm an actor myself.

JIM: *(Getting closer to him.)* Really?

RAY: Yes.

JIM: You've been in movies, too?

RAY: TV.

JIM: TV?

RAY: And some small parts in movies.

JIM: Really?

RAY: Wanna dance?

JIM: Dance?

A tango is heard at a low volume as RAY holds JIM in a dance position. Facing front, RAY moves sinuously in an eccentric and bizarre manner; then he stops.

RAY: *(Indicating towards the right.)*: Is there anybody in there?

JIM: In the office?

RAY: Uh-huh.

JIM: No.

They dance right as the volume of the music increases, and exit. A moment later, offstage, JIM lets out a sound of half-pain and half-pleasure. RAY enters, wiping his hands with a gray cloth, and stands in the same spot where he stood earlier. The music fades.

Dream b: A projection reads: "At the bathroom door." RAY faces the door and leans on it. Both his hands are on the doorknob. His head leans against the mirror. She is behind the door.

SHE: Do you think I'm one of those exotic flowers?

RAY: Don't you fuck with me again!

SHE: Do you think I'm going to sit in my place waiting for you with my little legs crossed while you fuck half the world!

RAY: You're going to stay in there till you change your mind! You hear! *(He presses his lips against his own image and moves his pelvis against the mirror.)*

SHE: Who's going to change his mind, you son of a bitch! You open up, or I'll cut you up in little pieces when I get out! *(Pause.)* Open up!

Ray reaches climax.

RAY: Ahhh … !

SHE: What are you doing!

RAY: Ahhh …

SHE: What are you doing?

RAY: Shut up!

"Harbor Lights" is heard.

Dream c: A projection reads: "On the fire escape." RAY sits on the fire escape. He looks out over the roofs.

RAY : *(Singing.)* Tra tra tra ta ta-ta. *(He looks at his shoe.)* Tra tra tra ta ta-ta. I have to shine my shoes. *(Short pause.)* Honey!

LORRAINE: *(Offstage.)* What?

Short pause.

RAY: Measure my cock.

LORRAINE: *(Offstage.)* Get off it!

RAY : *(Singing.)* Tra tra tra ta ta-ta.

LORRAINE enters and sits on the box.

LORRAINE: Do you know why they call me Mary?

RAY: What else should they call you?

LORRAINE: By my real name.

RAY: What's your real name?

LORRAINE: Lorraine. Mary's a nickname.

RAY: For Lorraine?

LORRAINE: Yup.

RAY: Like "Lefty"?

LORRAINE: What do you mean, like "Lefty"?

RAY: It's a nickname.

LORRAINE: For what?

RAY: For nothing. For an arm—

LORRAINE: I'll be darned.

RAY: So why do they call you Mary?

LORRAINE: For Mary Magdalene.

RAY: Why?

LORRAINE: Because of how ... *(Pointing with her head to his feet.)* ... you know.

RAY: What?

Lorraine: *(Pointing with her head.)* You know ... I ...

RAY: What?

LORRAINE: You know ... feet.

RAY: Oh yeah ... sweety, do my feet while I sing.

LORRAINE: You want?

RAY: Yeah. *(He sings and starts to take off his shoes.)* Ta ta ta ta ta-ta. Ta ta ta ta ta-ta. *(He looks at the roofs.)* Jesus Christ, everyone's fucking tonight.

The following occurs simultaneously: Fake Chinese music is heard; color lights whirl all over the stage; the window of the Chinese restaurant is lowered; a table is brought up center on the lower level; a chair is placed on the down side of the table, facing up.

Dream d: A projection reads: "In a Chinese restaurant." RAY sits at the table facing up. He wears an embroidered Chinese robe. He wears a long, narrow, white beard held on by white strings, and a bald cap with some scraggly hair around the edges. He is holding an open menu. He looks out the window at the GIRL, who is playing with a stick, cupped at the end, with a ball attached by a string. On the upstage side of the window, WANG stands to RAY's left. He also wears a narrow white false beard and a bald cap. He looks outside. Crows land on the pavement. The GIRL shoos them. When RAY and WANG speak, they move their mouths and WING's voice is heard. When WING speaks, she moves her mouth and WANG's voice is heard. Each time RAY speaks, he moves his head and torso in a manner resembling a mechanical toy. WANG moves his arms and legs up and down and makes sounds to express anger.

WANG: They leave home too young.

RAY: Who does?

WANG: The young.

RAY looks at the GIRL with a fiendish smile.

RAY: *(Laughing.)* Huh huh huh huh huh huh. Ya ya ya ya ya.

WANG: ... What was that ... ?

RAY looks at WANG. Then he looks at the GIRL and slurps. WANG is annoyed.

WANG: You leady to oldel? You look at the gill all night?

RAY looks at the menu closely and makes slurping sounds. WING enters upstage of the window. She writes, "Merry Xmas," and draws a bird and snow using a spray can on the window. RAY chews on the menu.

WANG: Now you eat menu! You-oldel-food!

RAY: What do you have? *(He makes slurping sounds.)*

WANG: *(Pointing to the menu.)* It's in menu!

RAY licks the menu.

WANG: Don't eat menu! Lead menu.

RAY makes sounds resembling Chinese as he moves his head from left to right. WANG indicates with head as he speaks.

WANG: You don't lead flom side to side! You lead up and down!

WANG turns the menu on the side. RAY's head vibrates and moves up and down as he continues making sounds resembling Chinese. WANG takes the menu from RAY. He opens it and looks at it.

WANG: We have hundled-yeal-old egg.

RAY belches.

WANG: Okay. We have fish fin soup.

RAY translates what WANG said into sounds that resemble Chinese. Then he belches.

WANG: Why you go like that?

RAY makes throwing up sounds. WANG wipes the table.

WANG: You have no table mannel.

RAY laps his tongue. WANG looks at the menu again.

WANG: Okay. We have Chinese pickle vegetable.

RAY starts to speak words resembling Chinese. He coughs. WANG pats him on the back and points to the window.

WANG: Chlistmas.

VOICE OVER: There are Chinese voices singing "Jingle Bells." Snow starts falling on the GIRL. RAY stretches his arms toward the window and starts to stand. The GIRL looks at RAY for a while through the window while snow falls on her. She enters the restaurant.

GIRL: Someone was accidentally wounded.

RAY stands, puts his head on the GIRL's chest, and slurps. WING enters the restaurant and looks at the window. RAY cries. The GIRL helps RAY to the chair.

WING: *(Pointing to the window.)* The bild didn't come out light. This little wing is sholtel than this little wing. And the little left leg of the little bild is not as good as the little light leg. And this little "a" is not good. We have to fix it.

WANG: Wing is sad. She failed. At the picture.

Crows alight. The GIRL runs outside. The following occurs simultaneously: Music is heard; colored lights whirl; the BOY enters up right, walks to the center, and turns front. There is a crow on his shoulder. He carries a tray with four lit candles. WANG goes up the left steps, takes the box from the right and a candle from the tray, and stands to the right of the BOY facing left. RAY stands and pretends to lose his balance. The GIRL puts her arms around him to support him. He puts his lips to her neck, his head drops to her chest, his hand drops to her buttocks as they go up the right steps. The GIRL takes a candle. RAY and the GIRL stand left of WING facing left. They all walk around the window to the main platform. WANG places his box down center while WING places hers two feet up of WANG's. They take paper bags from the boxes. The BOY places the tray on the downstage box. WING, WANG, and the GIRL place their candles on the tray. The GIRL helps RAY sit on the upstage box. WING and WANG stand behind RAY. The BOY stands down left, and the GIRL stands down right.

Dream e: A projection reads: "In the basement." The BOY *takes two hundred-dollar bills from his pocket and holds one in each hand. The* VOICE OVER *continues.*

WANG: He's going to buln the money.

The Boy lights both bills and lets them burn. Ray contorts and convulses.

RAY: Buln money? Buln money? Buln money? *(Pulling his hair.)* Can't beal it! Can't beal it! Can't beal it! Why? Why?

WANG: Yes.

RAY: Why buln money?

WANG: Is a leligious act. Not to explain.

RAY: *(His left hand is holding his right hand back, and his right hand is resisting.)* Difficult for me to watch. *(He tries to pull his eyelids open. His right hand takes his left hand and puts it in his pocket. He puts the right hand in his pocket.)* Difficult to keep hands in pocket. Difficult not to knock down boy! Put out file! Glab money!

WANG: Vely difficult.

The BOY *holds the crow towards* RAY. WING *and* WANG *flap their paper bags to create the sound of flapping wings.*

BOY: *(Imitating the sound of a crow.)* Take me to him! Take me to him! Take me to him!

The BOY *steps closer to* RAY, *holding the crow up.* RAY's *eyes open wide.*

BOY: I resemble him! He is like my mirror. He is like my mirror! I am like him! Take me to him!

RAY *touches his chin, nose, ears, eyes.*

BOY: Take me to him! Take me to him!

The crow starts pecking at RAY's *face.* RAY *covers his chin, nose, ears, eyes.*

BOY: Take me to him! Take me to him! Take me to him!

Music is heard. Lights whirl all over the stage. RAY *exits up right.* WANG, WING, *the* BOY, *and the* GIRL *hurry to the back. They scatter and run back and forth on the platform.* WING *and* WANG *flap their wings as if invisible crows are attacking from above. In the meantime, the set is restored to its position at the start of Lust.*

Dream f: In the streets of Bolivia. A projection reads: "In Bolivia." Music still plays. Lights still whirl. RAY enters left running. He wears a suit jacket. He joins the others in their running. When the set is restored, the others exit. RAY runs back and forth a few more times.

Scene 7

In RAY and HELENA's bedroom. HELENA is lying in bed. RAY stands right, facing right. He is in shirtsleeves looking in an imaginary mirror as he combs his hair and puts on a necktie.

HELENA: I was with a young boy.

RAY: You were?

HELENA: I already mentioned it to you.

RAY: So what about it?

HELENA: I was with him intimately.

RAY: So what about it?

HELENA: He asked me if I was sick.

RAY: He didn't use a condom?

HELENA: He did, but I asked him to kiss me.

RAY does not answer.

HELENA: I asked him to kiss me. *(Pause.)* Ray, I asked him to kiss me.

RAY: Yes, I heard you.

HELENA: He asked me if I was sick.

RAY: What did he mean?

HELENA: A venereal disease. *(Pause.)* I thought it should be I who asked.

RAY: Asked what?

HELENA: If he was sick.

RAY: *(Putting on his jacket.)* I agree with you. If you sleep with a whore, you should ask if he's sick.

HELENA: But instead, it was he who asked me.

RAY: It's you who should've asked him—because you sleep with whores.

HELENA: I'm not a whore, Ray.

RAY: I know. I said you sleep with whores.

HELENA: You know why I do it.

He walks to the up-chair.

RAY: You could have a venereal disease.

HELENA: Do you think I have a venereal disease?

RAY: I think you should be tested.

HELENA: That's humiliating. It's humiliating to have you think that of me.

RAY: You should be tested. You could have a venereal disease.

HELENA: You think that boy is right, then? You think he has a right to ask me if I'm sick when he's a whore? You think I could have a venereal disease?

RAY: You could.

Scene 8

In RAY and HELENA's bedroom. HELENA stands by the bed, holding a dress. BIRDIE sits on the downstage easy chair. There are several dresses on the bed and on the floor.

HELENA: ... What would you like to eat?

BIRDIE: Nothing, thank you.

They pick up the dresses. HELENA looks at one of the buttons on a dress.

HELENA: This one here is too big.

BIRDIE: What is?

Helena: Well, the button, or maybe the buttonhole is too small. The buttons are all the same, I think. The buttonhole is too small. I already had one fixed. I don't know if I can do anything about it now.

BIRDIE: Maybe you can get a smaller button.

HELENA: That wouldn't look right. *(Sitting on the bed.)* It would look uneven to have a button smaller than all the rest.

BIRDIE: *(Standing.)* Can't you cut the ends? One end. *(Going to HELENA.)* All you have to do is cut one end and then stitch it.

Helena: What do you mean?

BIRDIE: *(Taking the dress and looking at the buttonhole.)* One corner of the stitch on the buttonhole.

HELENA: It's sewn too tight.

BIRDIE: If you get a pair of scissors with a very fine point, you could push it down between the threads and cut some of the threads. *(Returning the dress to HELENA.)* Do you have one of those cuticle scissors with a fine point?

HELENA: I don't have any scissors.

BIRDIE: None at all?

HELENA: *(Shaking her head.)* They don't let me have them.

There is a sound offstage. They both look in the direction of the sound, then at each other.

HELENA: How long have you known Ray?

BIRDIE: Not very long.

HELENA: Is he your lover?

BIRDIE: No.

HELENA: How did you meet him?

BIRDIE: I met him when he hired me.

HELENA stands still, holding the dress.

HELENA: How did he know you wanted the work?

BIRDIE: Someone sent me.

HELENA: Who did? An agency?

BIRDIE: A friend.

HELENA: What did he hire you for?

BIRDIE looks down.

HELENA: You can't tell me?

BIRDIE: To look after you.

HELENA: *(Walking around the bed to the right.)* Do you understand Ray? Do you understand him when he talks?

BIRDIE: No.

HELENA: Well. Now he wants me to meet his brother. He's going to bring his brother here, for me to meet him. He's found a brother, and he wants me to meet him.

BIRDIE makes a move to stand.

HELENA: You stay—Can you understand that? Why does he want me to meet him?—You can have that dress if you want.

BIRDIE: … Thank you …

HELENA: Helena—*(Putting the dress on the bed.)*—you can call me Helena. Why be formal? What's the point?—How does he know if he's really his brother? *(Returning to the left of the bed.)* How does he know if this Charlie's really his brother? He never even saw him. How does he know that he's not a crook?

BIRDIE: How does he know?

HELENA: He thinks he is.

RAY: *(Offstage.)* Helena!

HELENA: *(To BIRDIE.)* See?

RAY: *(Offstage.)* Helena!

HELENA: The way he speaks to me.

RAY: Are you here? Charlie's here. Would you come down?

HELENA goes to the entranceway.

HELENA: *(With a polite smile, as if he could see her.)* Your brother?

RAY: *(Offstage.)* Yes.—Please, come.

HELENA looks down at her dress, adjusts it, and adjusts her hair.

HELENA: *(To BIRDIE.)* Do I look all right?

BIRDIE: Yes.

HELENA: Do you hate me?

BIRDIE: No. I don't hate you at all.

HELENA goes to the door. She pauses.

HELENA: He's seen his mother, hasn't he? *(Walking down.)* I know he's seen his mother. I know he has. Didn't he mention it to you? Did he tell you anything about it? He doesn't tell me anything anymore. He doesn't want to talk to me.—You knew his mother, didn't you, Birdie? You knew Nadine.

BIRDIE: Yes.

HELENA: You're one of them, aren't you?

BIRDIE: Yes.

HELENA: You love him too, don't you?

BIRDIE lowers her head.

HELENA: I don't mind if you do. I feel sorry for you.

BIRDIE: I'm sorry.

HELENA: Don't be sorry for me, Birdie. Don't be sorry for me. I don't mind that you love him. You're not a bad person. I feel sorry for you.

BIRDIE cries. HELENA shakes her head.

HELENA: Poor soul.

Scene 9

In RAY and HELENA's bedroom. RAY is in bed. He wears an undershirt. BIRDIE enters. She stops at the door. She carries a cup of coffee. She takes a couple of steps down. He looks at her. She moves her hand with the coffee cup towards him.

RAY: I'll take it.

BIRDIE's hand starts to shake. The coffee cup rattles. Her arm stretches toward him. She takes a step toward him. She waits with her head down. He takes the coffee. She starts to exit.

RAY: Please wait.

BIRDIE stops.

RAY: Sit down.

BIRDIE sits. RAY drinks more coffee. He looks at her. She looks at him. He nods. She lowers her head.

BIRDIE: Yes.

The lights go to black. Then they come up. BIRDIE is straddling Ray. They make violent sounds.

Scene 10

In RAY and HELENA's bedroom. JOSEPH sits on the upstage easy chair. BIRDIE straightens the bed from the up left side of the bed and stands there through the rest of the scene. HELENA sits on the floor facing JOSEPH.

JOSEPH: I've never talked to you about the things that are important to me. I've never talked to you about my work. You may not realize what I do—because my work is not something you can see. It's in my head. My work is my life. It's my universe. I have not loved anything the way I love my work. I don't know that I could think of my life without it. I don't know that I could live without it. I don't know that I could exist without my work.

HELENA looks in the direction of the door. JOSEPH also looks. There is a pause.

JOSEPH: Come in, Ray.

RAY takes a step in.

JOSEPH: How are you?

RAY: I'm fine. *(He stands behind the straight chair.)*

JOSEPH: I believe Ray is taking over my business, Helena.

HELENA: Is he?

JOSEPH: Why don't you ask him?

HELENA looks at RAY. RAY looks away.

HELENA: *(To Joseph.)* What does this mean?

JOSEPH: It means he's taking over my business.

JOSEPH looks at RAY. RAY is still looking away.

JOSEPH: What do you say, Ray? *(Silence.)* Is there anything I can do to prevent it? Your taking my business from me? Taking everything away from me?

RAY looks at BIRDIE. He then sits on the straight chair.

JOSEPH: You have a cold heart, son. *(Pause.)* Well, I'll be going now. *(He stands.)* You are the master of your own life, Helena. *(There is a pause. He waits for a response.)* Exercise your free will. Animals can do better than you, Helena. Animals are not our slaves even if they appear to be. Even when they wag their tails, they're not dependent on us. We're not their masters, and they're not our slaves. Animals manage to work their way around us even if it appears that they are dependent on us.—They don't need to bemoan their lack of freedom.—We also don't need to bemoan our lack of freedom in regard to any other human being. *(Pause.)* Haven't I taught you to love yourself?

HELENA looks at JOSEPH.

HELENA: No,—Father. *(She looks down.)*

Scene 11

In JOSEPH's office. JOSEPH enters abruptly. He is visibly frightened. He opens the drawer of his desk and starts to look among his papers frantically. He hears a sound. He turns to the entranceway.

JOSEPH: Here they come.

RAY enters. JOSEPH reaches into his breast pocket. RAY rapidly moves to stop JOSEPH's action. They struggle. RAY pulls a gun from JOSEPH's hand. JOSEPH is shaking. He lowers his head. RAY puts his hand on JOSEPH's back affectionately.

JOSEPH: What a mistake I've made. What a mistake. What a mistake.

JOSEPH sits and rests his head on the desk. As the lights whirl, the following occurs simultaneously: The scenery is carried out; HELENA enters; RAY walks right. HELENA helps JOSEPH up. They walk around the stage. He is leaning on her and makes plaintive sounds. With HELENA's unnoticed help, his clothes come off his body as if they were peeling off. He becomes more and more debilitated, until he falls to the ground inert and naked but for his shorts.

Scene 12

HELENA walks to up center. RAY sits on a chair down right facing down. She looks at him.

HELENA: He told me he always wished for a son and not a daughter. That he loved me, but that he wanted a son. He said he wanted a son just like me because he loved me. He knew it was possible that a son could have resembled you instead of me. He said he knew his son could have been like you. That he could have been a misfit. A crazy son. Someone who, like you, is distasteful in every way. But he said that he still wished I had been a boy.

Hunger

CHARACTERS

CHARLIE: A portly man, seventy-six years old. He has a scar on his forehead. He is pensive. He seems to place the same value on all things. He wears a worn and stained suit and necktie.

BIRDIE: Seventy-four years old. She is inquisitive and reserved. She wears a black crepe dress and high-heeled black shoes, and carries a clutch purse.

RAY: Sixty-seven years old. He is high-strung and obsessed. He suffers from nervous ticks and tremors. He is in rags.

REBA: Fifty years old. Ray's mate. She is detached and pensive. She has a dry wisdom. She is in rags.

THE ANGEL: A stone-like gothic figure. One of his wings is broken and hangs behind him. He carries a wooden box containing animal entrails strapped around his neck.

After an economic disaster. Some time in the future.

A warehouse. Against the back wall there is a platform two-and-a-half feet tall, eight feet deep, and the width of the stage. At each end of the platform there are archways that lead to other rooms. On the platform there are two sets of steps, left and right, that lead to the stage. On the upstage end of each side wall there are archways that lead to other rooms.

Scene 1: Room 1

In the dark there is the sound of a bell struck at about six-second intervals. There is a desk and a chair up left, and a second chair against the center of the left wall. The lights are dim. CHARLIE enters left on the platform. He moves slowly. He takes a few steps and stops. BIRDIE's steps are heard. She enters. CHARLIE proceeds to walk in front of her. They reach the archway on the right and walk around to enter through the right archway on the floor level. CHARLIE stops halfway and lets BIRDIE proceed to the chair on the left.

CHARLIE: I'm sorry he's not here. He said he couldn't come today, that he didn't think he'd be here. That he had things to do.

BIRDIE: Did you tell him I was coming?

CHARLIE: Yes.

BIRDIE sits.

BIRDIE: What did you say?

CHARLIE: I said I wanted to see him.

BIRDIE: Did you tell him who I was?

CHARLIE: ... No.

BIRDIE: What did you tell him?

CHARLIE: *(Walking to the desk and sitting.)* I told him a woman had been here to see him. And he said he didn't think he'd be able to come.

BIRDIE: Did he say why?

CHARLIE: Yes. He said there were things he had to do.

BIRDIE: What?

CHARLIE: He said he had to look for things.

BIRDIE: What things?

CHARLIE: To exchange or to eat, or things to sell, or to use for himself. Sometimes he gets things he can sell.

BIRDIE: Where does he find these things?

CHARLIE: In the street. In the rubble. Empty buildings, I guess. I don't know. Maybe he burgles sometimes. Although I doubt that. He doesn't come up with anything too costly. He goes out at night. Hunting. Then he spends the day here. He sleeps or sits or paces, resting, waiting till it gets dark again to go out again. It's safer then.

BIRDIE: Safer?

CHARLIE: To go out. At night no one can see you. Not as easily.

BIRDIE: Stealing?

CHARLIE: Not stealing. I don't think he steals. He finds things. In the streets. In the rubble.

BIRDIE: What can he find?

CHARLIE: Many things. A piece of ribbon, a button, an old handle, a spool, nails, if they're not too crooked. Sometimes he's spotted something, a good pile, some place where he thinks there may be some stuff. But he doesn't go to it right away. He waits till dark.—It's too dangerous to do it in the daytime. If someone sees him looking and putting something in his pocket, he may be followed, and he may be jumped, hurt badly, if the person thinks he has found something of value— or killed. When you're in the street, you should never put anything in your pocket. If you do, someone may think you're carrying something of value.—Why are you looking for him?

BIRDIE: I was asked to talk to him.

CHARLIE: ... To talk to him?

BIRDIE: It seems he took something with him when he left the Compound.

CHARLIE: Did he?

BIRDIE: It seems that he did.

CHARLIE: What?

BIRDIE: I don't know. There's something he may have taken.

CHARLIE: I hope that if he took something, that he still has it, and that you want to buy it from him. If he has it, he'll sell it to you. I'm sure he will, if you want to buy it.—Then he may get back on his feet again. If what he has is worth something. He's sinking lower and lower. *(Pause.)* Once you're outside, you can't get in again. There's never a reason to go in. That is, one has a reason, but they don't see that you do. *(Pause.)* Once you're out, it is not likely they'll want you in. That's why you have to leave. *(Pause.)*

BIRDIE: Is Nadine here, Charlie?

CHARLIE: ... Nadine?

BIRDIE: Do you remember Nadine?

CHARLIE: Yes ... She's old. She doesn't remember things too well.—I think Nadine died.

BIRDIE: When?

CHARLIE: When?

BIRDIE: Did she die a long time ago? *(There is a silence.)* You don't remember things too well, do you?

CHARLIE: What?

BIRDIE: Do you remember who you are?

CHARLIE: Not too well.

BIRDIE: You didn't remember me, did you—when you saw me.

CHARLIE: No, I didn't.

BIRDIE: And now, do you know who I am?

CHARLIE: No.—Things are very different now. I don't think that much any-more. Not often. I was hit on the head when I was little. *(Pause.)* A moment ago I was thinking I used to be skinny. Was I?

BIRDIE: Yes.

CHARLIE: Did you know me before?

BIRDIE: Yes.

CHARLIE: It's different now. The way a person thinks. The way a person is.

BIRDIE: Yes.

CHARLIE: Who'd believe that I'd end up having a good position. I've gone far, and I never thought I would. And yet Ray, who went so far when he was young, is scrambling for a piece of bread. Do you know that?

BIRDIE: *(Standing and walking left.)* Yes.

CHARLIE: Did you know him then?

BIRDIE: *(Walking toward the desk.)* Yes.—

CHARLIE: Did you know him well?

BIRDIE: Yes.—

CHARLIE: Did you know me?

BIRDIE: Yes.—Do you help him now?

CHARLIE: Who?

BIRDIE: Ray.

CHARLIE: … What do you mean?

BIRDIE: Do you help Ray? Do you give him something now and then?

CHARLIE: Ray?

BIRDIE: Do you give him food?

CHARLIE: No.

BIRDIE: Why not?

CHARLIE: I don't have that much to give.

BIRDIE: He's your brother.

Pause.

CHARLIE: Is he? I don't remember that.

BIRDIE: Ray is your brother.

CHARLIE: I remember Rainbow. Did you know her?

BIRDIE: Yes, I knew her once.

CHARLIE: Ray met Rainbow once.

BIRDIE: He did?

CHARLIE: Yes. He didn't know she was his sister. Did she know she was his sister?

BIRDIE: I don't know.

CHARLIE: Did you know me?

BIRDIE: Yes, Charlie.

CHARLIE: It's harder for some.

BIRDIE: What is?

CHARLIE: To settle down. When is he going to settle down? It's harder for Ray. It's taken him too long.—He's never quiet. He's never quiet at all. He's too restless. Sometimes he doesn't even come to sleep. He stays up all night. *(He puts his hand to his forehead.)* Someone hit me on the head, and it still hurts sometimes. *(He stands and walks right.)* Sometimes he comes up in the middle of the night, and he wakes up everyone. He sleeps in the daytime, but the others sleep at night and he doesn't let them sleep.

BIRDIE *looks around the room.*

BIRDIE: What do you do here, Charlie?—What is your work?

CHARLIE: My work? I look after the place. I see to it that things are in order. There's always a problem ... sometimes. Sometimes someone wants to get in. Someone who doesn't belong.—I see to it that they don't get in.

Sometimes there are fights among the people who live here. *(He walks toward the desk.)*

BIRDIE: Do you receive payment for your work?

CHARLIE: Why do you want to know?

BIRDIE: ... I don't know how things work here.

CHARLIE: I get paid in goods. Some food. Sometimes. I got this suit.

BIRDIE: How do the others live?

CHARLIE: We get food ... sometimes. *(Pause.)* You talk different. You don't sound like anyone I know. Your voice sounds different. The color of your skin is different. You are of a different time. *(He walks to her. He takes her hand. Her purse falls to the floor. He examines her hand.)* Your hand is like an object of art. Why is your skin so perfect? What is it made of?

BIRDIE touches the side of CHARLIE's face.

BIRDIE: ... Charlie ...

CHARLIE: *(Putting his arm around her waist and bringing her body against his.)* I would like to know what it feels like to put my body against yours. I knew you'd feel fresh. Like water. Like I've had you in my arms.

She moves away from him gently.

BIRDIE: Please don't.

He releases her. She takes a few steps back. He lowers his head in shame. He picks up her purse and hands it to her. He returns to the desk, sits down, folds his arms on the desk, and rests his head on his arms. She takes a photograph from her purse, walks to him, and puts the photograph on the desk. She puts her hand on his back.

BIRDIE: Look at this.—

He starts to look up.

BIRDIE: Do you remember this?

He takes the picture and looks at it. His mind travels through time.

CHARLIE: A picture ... *(He puts the picture down. His head starts to move down again.)* Would you like to take a nap now? I'm very tired. I would like to rest.

WHAT OF THE NIGHT? ○ 161

He rests his head on his arms. She slides the picture towards her and looks at it.

BIRDIE: *(Putting her hand on his head.)* Yes, Charlie. You rest. *(She puts the picture in her purse.)* I'll come back later.

Scene 2: Room 2

The same structure as the first. There are bodies shrouded in blankets lying down or sitting against the walls. RAY and REBA lie center right. They are covered with blankets. He holds a cloth sack that contains several small objects he has collected in the street. He mumbles.

RAY: Why wouldn't it work?

Pause.

REBA: What?

RAY: It would work.

REBA: What?

Pause.

RAY: Reba, I told you time and time again.

REBA: I forgot.

RAY: *(Hurt.)* Reba ... *(Pause.)* ... You forgot? *(Pause.)* ... How could you forget?

REBA: I don't know, Ray.

RAY: It didn't matter to you?

REBA: It did.

RAY: How could you forget?

REBA: I had other things on my mind.

RAY: Other things?

REBA: Other thoughts.

RAY: What thoughts, Reba?

REBA: Different thoughts.

RAY: Like what, Reba?

REBA: They change, Ray.

RAY: Every day?

REBA: Not every day of the year, but there are a few things that I think about, and I think about them on different days.

RAY: You don't remember the things I tell you?

REBA: I know there are things you tell me, but I don't remember them from day to day.

RAY: You don't remember the things I dream about?

REBA: I know there are some things you dream about, but I don't remember what they are.

RAY: How could you forget those things I want—and dream of?

REBA: It's been a while since we last talked about them.

RAY: How long?

REBA: I don't remember.

RAY: I thought you loved me, and I thought to love a person is to know what their dreams are, and the things they think about. And that thinking about those things makes the person get through each day. And I thought to love a person is to know those things and to think of those things, too, and to know when the person is thinking of those things. (*He empties the contents of the sack on the floor: a stone, a piece of wood, a bottle top, and a piece of metal. He lines up two pieces on the floor and holds the other two.*) Look at this, Reba. You see this? (*Pointing at the pieces.*) This is you. This is me. (*He picks up the pieces and gives* REBA *her piece. Then, as he puts a third piece down.*) This person comes and puts his piece down. Then you come and you put your piece down.—Put it down.

She puts her piece down.

RAY: (*Putting his own piece down.*) Then I come and I put my piece down. This person is first, you're second, and I'm third. We can go sit in the sun, or go for a walk, or do something we have to do. When it's time to come in the shelter, we stand in line. Like this. We know our place because we know what our piece is. You see what I mean?—Reba, do you see what I mean?—This here is me … this is Nadine … This is Helena … This is

Birdie … This is Rainbow … *(He starts to cry.)* This is Helena. *(Pause.)* Helena … poor Helena.

CHARLIE enters from the up right archway. He carries a clipboard with a printed form. A pencil and an eraser are attached to the clipboard by strings. He stops to write on the form.

RAY: … Charlie, *(Pause.)* look at this.

Charlie moves closer and looks at the piece.

RAY: This is what I wanted to show you. This is what I was talking to you about. *(Pointing.)* This is someone who came first. This is Reba. This represents her. This is me, and this is someone else.

CHARLIE sits down. RAY waits a moment for CHARLIE's reply.

RAY: Charlie, someone comes first and puts his piece down. Then Reba comes and puts her piece down. She's second. Then, I come and put my piece down. Then, someone else puts his piece down. It's clear in what order we came in. We don't have to stand in line. We can go somewhere else, sit down someplace, or do something we have to do. Then when it's time to come in, we stand in line in the order of our pieces. *(Pause.)* See?—A person may have to go to the toilet. They can go to the toilet and come back, because their piece is on the floor in place. When your piece is on the floor, it means you're around and you're coming back.

CHARLIE looks at the pieces.

RAY: This is what I was telling you about: a way to save us from standing in line. You see what I mean.

CHARLIE looks at the pieces.

RAY: Charlie, it's a way for us not to have to wait in line such a long time.

CHARLIE: I don't have a form for that, Ray.

REBA: I didn't think it was going to work, Ray. I didn't tell you because I didn't want to say when I wasn't sure. But I didn't think it was going to work. Things like that don't usually work. I don't know why, but they usually don't work. *(She sits up. Her arm is in a sling.)* You see, my arm is broken. I think my arm is broken. Last week I fell and I hit my elbow. Now it hurts. I put it in a sling because it doesn't hurt as much if I keep it like this. If it hangs, it hurts. But I need help, because it may be broken. And I wondered, Charlie, if I could get some help.

CHARLIE: What kind of help?

REBA: I thought that I might get some food because I'm disabled, or that I might get something to make a cast.

CHARLIE: ... With plaster?

REBA: Or some sticks and gauze to make a splint.

CHARLIE: You want me to put in a requisition?

REBA: Might as well.

CHARLIE writes on the form.

REBA: Are you going to put my name on that?

CHARLIE continues writing.

CHARLIE: You have to sign this.

REBA: ... I don't know, Charlie.

CHARLIE continues writing, then hands the clipboard to REBA. She takes the clipboard and looks at the form.

RAY: *(Pointing to the objects on the floor.)* Are you going to put in a requisition for this?

CHARLIE: I don't know Ray ... I don't know what kind of forms you'd use for this kind of thing. That requisition would not go on this form. You have to have a form that has the right questions.

REBA: I'd prefer it if you didn't put my name on this.

CHARLIE: What do you mean?

REBA: *(Handing the clipboard to CHARLIE.)* My name here, Charlie.

CHARLIE: Well, I can't put in this requisition unless I put your name on it.

REBA: I don't like to have my name on that paper. I don't like it when my name is down on paper. It's better if you don't put my name there. Don't put your name down on paper. If you see something happen, you say you didn't see it. And if you didn't see it, you say you saw it. It's better that way. Always say the opposite. Otherwise they think you're lying. If you lie, you sound better to them. You don't sound so stupid to them. People don't like it when you tell the truth. You can't go inside anyplace if you tell the truth. If you tell the truth, you have to stay outside. They don't let you in. You stay in the cold. They won't let you through the door. If you tell the truth, you end up arrested.

CHARLIE: *(Annoyed.)* What do I do with this now?

REBA: I don't know, Charlie.

CHARLIE: You have to sign it.

REBA shakes her head.

CHARLIE: Didn't you know you had to sign a requisition?

REBA: No, I didn't know that.

CHARLIE: You never made one before?

REBA shakes her head.

CHARLIE: You did, Reba.

REBA: When?

CHARLIE looks at the clipboard.

CHARLIE: You have. I know you have.

REBA: No, Charlie.

CHARLIE: You better sign it.

REBA: No, Charlie.

CHARLIE: I know you have.—Now I'm going to have to erase this.

He erases what he wrote and starts to walk left. BIRDIE walks into the archway to the left. She carries a shopping sack and a loaf of bread. CHARLIE stops and looks at her for a moment.

CHARLIE: Here's that woman, Ray.

RAY turns to look at her.

CHARLIE: She's looking for you. Do you know her? (*CHARLIE walks to BIRDIE.*) Ray's here.

CHARLIE exits. BIRDIE crosses to the right and stands against the wall.

BIRDIE: Now they're calm, but something is seething inside them. Something that may ignite without much provocation. Something swelling inside them. I feel the stench in the air. I must be careful. I must not provoke their rage. I must not let them notice I'm different from them. If they do, I'm sure they'll blame me. What's happening to them is not my fault.

How could it be? If they think it is, they will vent their rage on me. I must be careful. *(She walks to RAY and REBA.)* Ray ...

RAY: How are you, Birdie?

BIRDIE: I'm fine.

RAY: I'm going back soon. I've been getting ready to go to the Compound. I've been working on some ideas. Some people blow their wad, but I haven't. I assure you, Birdie, I have some very good ideas. I'm going back soon. I'm sure they'll appreciate my going back. Because I've had time to work on some ideas that are of value. Useful.

BIRDIE: I brought you some food.

RAY: Thank you. This is Reba.

BIRDIE sits.

BIRDIE: Hello, Reba.

REBA: Pleased to meet you.

BIRDIE hands the shopping sack to RAY.

BIRDIE: This is for you. It's still hot.

RAY: Thank you.

BIRDIE breaks the loaf of bread in half.

BIRDIE: *(As she hands a piece to RAY.)* Here is some bread.

RAY: Thank you.

REBA starts to walk to the up left archway.

BIRDIE: I'm going to take this to Charlie.

RAY: Why him?

REBA stops.

BIRDIE: Why not?

RAY: Why is the bigger piece for him?

BIRDIE: I didn't realize it was bigger.

RAY: You're lying.

Birdie: Me? *(She turns to him.)* Why would I?

RAY: How could you not know which piece is bigger?

BIRDIE: I didn't notice.

RAY: That's a lie.

BIRDIE: *(Coming closer.)* Why do you say that?

RAY: The way you say, "I'm going to bring him this," or, "This is for him."

BIRDIE sits.

RAY: The way you say, "This is for him," as if you care for him more than you care for me. While before you used to say how I did this or that better than him. Now you want to bring him the bigger piece. As if you still care for him. Because he has a better position.

BIRDIE: *(As she exchanges the pieces of bread.)* Take this one. *(As she turns upstage.)* I'll bring him the smaller piece. *(Walking to the up left archway.)* I did it without thinking.

When RAY speaks, BIRDIE stops without turning.

RAY: *(Hysterically.)* You didn't do anything without thinking, Birdie! You think about everything!

BIRDIE: *(As she exits.)* That's how you always used to talk.

RAY: *(Shouting.)* I think about you each day! *(Turning front and sobbing.)* I think about her each day!

RAY sobs. He moves to the down left corner carrying the sack and bread as he sobs. His movements resemble those of a monkey. When he reaches the wall, his sounds become louder, more plaintive, like a torn animal. BIRDIE reenters.

REBA: That doesn't matter anymore, Ray. You can't think about those things anymore.—He has to forget that. We all have to forget where we came from. I can't remember where I came from. I have a hard time remembering that.—Sit down, Birdie.

BIRDIE sits.

REBA: Make yourself at home. You're among friends. You're welcome here.

CHARLIE enters carrying a folded blanket.

CHARLIE: *(Offering BIRDIE the blanket.)* This is for you, Birdie. To keep you warm.

BIRDIE stares at the blanket. CHARLIE puts the blanket on her lap. She pushes it off her lap and looks at REBA. CHARLIE picks up the blanket. BIRDIE moves up right. CHARLIE moves towards her, offering her the blanket. She takes a few steps backwards. She then runs around him and stands next to REBA. REBA holds her hand. There is the sound of a bell.

REBA: It's time for our rations. *(She stands. She turns to Ray.)*

CHARLIE: Come, Ray. It's time for our rations.

RAY joins them. They walk upstage left and turn to face right. The ANGEL enters from the up right archway. He walks, shuffling his feet with short wide steps. When the ANGEL reaches center right, they walk to the ANGEL. They stand facing him in a semicircle.

REBA: Soon you'll feel like us. It won't take too long. A moment ago you felt you were different. But it won't take too long before you feel just like us.

All but BIRDIE kneel. The ANGEL empties the contents of a box on the floor.

REBA: Come, eat something.

BIRDIE kneels on the floor as REBA, CHARLIE, and Ray bow their heads. BIRDIE gags and faints. The ANGEL begins to exit.

REBA: She fainted. She's not used to this.— *(To the ANGEL.)* Next time would you bring her something she can eat? Something she likes. *(To BIRDIE.)* What would you like? *(To the ANGEL, who continues walking.)* Bring her some bread and coffee and some juice and cream! Cheese and crackers instead of bread. And some fruit! I think fruit is good—when you feel the way she does—listless. She feels very weak. Perhaps she should have some red meat. Some roast beef!—Rare! So it puts some blood into her system. And some milk.—She should not have sugar, because that isn't good for you. But she should have honey, which is good for you. And I think she should have something hot. Instead of coffee she should have something more nourishing! Pea soup, or perhaps chicken soup is more digestible. With potatoes, because the starch of the potato will restore some of her lost strength!—And fish. Fish is good for the brain, because when you faint the brain feels as if it's disintegrating—either baked, or a fried patty, or some tuna and canned sardines. She should have some vegetables, carrot sticks! And raw cauliflower! Or any raw vegetables they may have! Although cooked vegetables are also good! If they are not overcooked! And also a little red wine. I understand it's good to pick you up. Or sherry's better, I think. It is better to pick you up. *(To BIRDIE, softly.)* Would you like a little liqueur?

RAY turns to BIRDIE sobbing. He stretches his arm to her. His head starts coming up as he's sobbing. He looks up to the heavens. He is now wailing. The lights fade to black. The bell is heard once.

Enter THE NIGHT

★ ★ ★ ★ ★ ★ ★ ★ ★ ★ ★

Enter THE NIGHT premiered at the New City Theater, Seattle, Washington, on April 16, 1993.

CAST

TRESSA, Mary Ewald
PAULA, Patricia Mattick
JACK, Brian Faker

Written during the author's tenure of a Lila Wallace Literary Fellowship.

Maria Irene Fornes, DIRECTOR

Donald Eastman, SET DESIGNER
Anne Militello, LIGHTING DESIGNER
Rose Pendleton, COSTUME DESIGNER

An empty warehouse or barn. The downstage area has been turned into a living space. In the center there is a pit, as large as the space permits. On the down side of the pit there is railing and stairs that lead to the floor below. On both sides of the pit there are planks that lead to the upstage area. On the down left area there is the entrance to a bathroom, a kitchen, and TRESSA's *bedroom.*

Center stage, down of the railing, there is a bench that will serve as a bed. On the right there is a table and four chairs. On the upstage side of the pit there is another bench that also serves as a bed. On the upstage right of the bench there is a folding screen, and to the left there is an armchair. Upstage of the screen there is a kitchen.

Downstage left there is a small table (table 2) with a chair facing upstage. To the right of the table there is a carpenter's cabinet. At the start, one of its drawers is open. On top of the cabinet there is a cassette player and a table mirror.

The characters quote from the novel Lost Horizon *by James Hilton. The voice of the* HIGH LAMA *in the last scene is that of Sam Jaffe in Frank Capra's film* Lost Horizon.

★ ACT ONE

The stage lights are very dim. A car is heard stopping outside. There is the sound of a car door opening and closing. The lights of dawn are seen on the wall stage right as the doors below open. Steps are heard. A light is turned on downstairs. TRESSA *is seen coming up the steps. She wears a light coat over a dress and white oxford shoes. She carries a purse over her shoulder and a nurse's uniform over her arm. She walks to a light switch and turns on a dim overhead light. She walks to the table, takes a notebook and pencil from her purse, and lays them on the table. She walks to the upstage area, taking the purse and uniform with her. On the way there, she leans over* PAULA, *who is asleep on the upper bench, and gently pulls the covers over her shoulders. She then walks to the cassette player and turns it on. Billie Holiday's "Don't Explain" is heard. She walks behind the screen, hangs the purse and uniform on it. She takes off her coat, shoes, stockings, and dress, puts on an undershirt, puts on the pants of a blue cotton Chinese worker's outfit, puts on plain Chinese black slippers and a Chinese worker's jacket. She walks down and left to the kitchen, then reenters with a cup of coffee and walks to the table. She turns on the overhead lamp, sits, and goes over her notes, pencil in hand. In the course of her reading she makes some pencil corrections.*

TRESSA:

6 p.m.	Patient in bed. Intermittent cough. Fogger in use. Skin very dry. Lotion applied to extremities.
8:30	Patient raising green phlegm periodically. Fluids not accepted.

11:00	Dr. Winternits in to visit. Heparin lock d/c.
3 a.m.	Patient incontinent of large amount of formed soft yellow BM. Decubitus care given. Mycitracin ointment to skin on buttocks.
3:30	Massage applied to legs. Elastic stockings replaced. /c legs elevated.
6:00	Patient resting in bed at this time. Relieved by Nurse Becker.

Tressa Harris, RN.

She turns to look in the direction of PAULA; *she turns back and leans her head on her hands for a moment. She takes a drink of coffee and walks left, taking the cup of coffee with her. She stops at the light switch and turns on the light on the left of the upper platform. She sits in the chair on the upper platform.*

PAULA: *(Half asleep.)* Who's there?

TRESSA: It's me.

PAULA: Oh, you scared me.

TRESSA goes to PAULA.

TRESSA: *(Touching PAULA's face.)* It's just me.

TRESSA starts walking down.

PAULA: Someone came in a while ago.

Tressa: Who?

PAULA: He was standing there, looking in the drawer.

TRESSA: Which drawer?

PAULA: That one.—It's open.

TRESSA walks to the drawer.

TRESSA: Who was it?

PAULA: *(Pointing to the cabinet.)* He was standing there, where you are.

TRESSA starts walking up.

PAULA: He said he wasn't a thief. That he needed something, and you told him to get it.

TRESSA: *(Turning to look at the drawer.)* What was it he needed?

PAULA: A tool.

TRESSA: What tool?

PAULA: He didn't say.

TRESSA: *(Walking toward the drawer.)* And where was he looking for that tool?

PAULA: In that drawer.—It's open.

TRESSA leans over the drawer.

TRESSA: There are no tools in that drawer.

PAULA: Well, that's the one he was looking in. *(Short pause.)*

TRESSA: What was the tool for?

PAULA: He didn't say.

TRESSA walks to the up left chair and sits.

TRESSA: How did he get in?

PAULA: I don't know.

TRESSA looks in the direction of the drawer.

TRESSA: Did he take anything?

PAULA: Not that I know.

TRESSA: What did he look like?

PAULA: He was short. He had long shiny straight hair like a Latin. He wore baggy pants that went up to his chest like a zoot suit. He wore suspenders. And a white shirt. And he was very clean. That's why I wasn't scared. As if murderers couldn't be clean. He had a big moustache and a big nose. He said his name was José Luis. Do you know any José Luis?

TRESSA: That must've been Jack.

PAULA: Jack? Why would Jack come in dressed like that?

TRESSA: To be funny.

PAULA: It wasn't Jack. You think I wouldn't recognize Jack?

TRESSA: What happened then?

PAULA: He sat there where you're sitting.

TRESSA: He did?

PAULA: Yes.

TRESSA: And then?

PAULA: He said he couldn't possibly marry me.

TRESSA: That sounds like Jack.

PAULA: It wasn't Jack.

TRESSA: What made him say that?

PAULA: I don't know. I never said he should.—Then he said, "Look at me. Hairs growing out of my nostrils. A mustache. Look at my mustache. Look at my gold tooth. I'm a short guy. Why should I marry you?" Then he leaned forward and said, "Do your legs want to wrap themselves around me?" I said, "Sure."

TRESSA: What?

PAULA: I lost my sense of judgment. It didn't matter to me who I wrapped my legs around.

TRESSA: Paula!

PAULA: I'm kidding. I wasn't awake.—He said, "Okay."

PAULA *shrugs her shoulders.* TRESSA *laughs.*

TRESSA: What happened then?

PAULA: I don't know.

TRESSA: You dreamt it.

PAULA *shrugs again.*

TRESSA: You want coffee? *(She starts to go to the left ramp.)*

PAULA: *(Walking down the right ramp.)* I'll get it.

TRESSA: I'll get it. *(As she exits left.)* Anything else happen while I was gone?

PAULA: Pete called.

TRESSA: He misses you?

PAULA: I guess. He wanted to see if I got in okay. And to say he was okay.

TRESSA: That's nice. How is he?

PAULA: He's fine.

TRESSA: Good. Did Jack call?

PAULA: No.

TRESSA: He's coming.

PAULA: He is? When?

TRESSA: Early. He said early. He can't wait to see you. He's bringing crois-sants. *(She exits left.)*

PAULA: Are you staying up?

TRESSA: Yes. I'm wide awake.

PAULA: How's your patient?

TRESSA: Not good. He was in pain.

PAULA: Did you get any rest?

TRESSA: *(Entering with a cup of coffee for PAULA.)* No. *(Pause.)* I think he's going to die.

PAULA: Will he go to the hospital?

TRESSA: He wants to stay home. *(She gives PAULA the coffee and returns to the up left chair.)*

PAULA: Why?

TRESSA: I think he's given up.

PAULA: You can't save him?

TRESSA: Me? Save him?

PAULA: *(Standing and opening her arms.)* I always think when I'm about to die I'll call your name, and you'll run to my side and save me. You'll just put your hand on my forehead, and I'll get well.

TRESSA: Sure, that's what we nurses do.

PAULA: That's right.

PAULA walks to TRESSA, puts her arm around her, and leans her head on TRESSA's.

PAULA: At least you.

PAULA goes to the bench and puts her blanket around her shoulders.

TRESSA: I just work hard making people comfortable …

PAULA walks down toward the table and sits.

TRESSA: … if possible. So they can bear their pain … their agony. If they get well, my work is rewarded. It's wonderful to see their first smile as they begin to feel better. And even more wonderful if that smile is directed at me. *(She walks down.)* When they begin to feel better, they feel you've been a partner in their cure because you've watched them at every step. They are grateful and appreciative for the help you've given them.

PAULA: And if they don't survive?

TRESSA: *(Walks to the table.)* If they don't survive, we feel a sense of loss. *(She sits.)* We've lost the battle.

PAULA: Have you lost the battle for Russell?

TRESSA: Yes, I think he wants to die.

TRESSA walks to the downstage bench and sits. She is despondent. PAULA walks to her and kisses her forehead.

PAULA: *You should rest, dear.*

TRESSA: I will. *(She exits left and speaks from offstage.)* You want anything?

PAULA: Like what?

TRESSA: Breakfast?

PAULA: No, thank you. I'm not ready to get up yet. I'm going back to bed. *(She starts to get into bed, reaches for her cup, and hands it to TRESSA.)* I'll have some more coffee though.

TRESSA: *(Goes to the kitchen. Offstage.)* So, how are things with you?

PAULA: All right, I suppose … *(She sits on the lower bench.)* The same.

TRESSA: *(Entering with a headband on and holding an open jar of yellowish white base, which she is applying to her face.)* What do you mean?

PAULA: *(Lying on the bench.)* I'm not well. But I don't pay any attention to it.

TRESSA: *(Going to the table left.)* What's wrong?

PAULA: I pretend I'm well. No one has told me that I'm well. But I act as if I am.

TRESSA starts walking to PAULA.

PAULA: As if I've been told by a doctor that I'm well, and I can go ahead and do whatever I want. Well, I haven't been told that. If I stop taking my heart pills, I'll die.

TRESSA: *(Going to the left side of the bench and kneeling.)* … Paula …

PAULA: Yes.—I keep doing the work on the farm, and I keep saying, "It's not going to harm me." I keep saying that. But there's a voice inside me that tells me, "If you keep doing what you're doing, you're going to die. The next shovel you push through the dirt will kill you." *(As if replying to herself.)* "This is good for me." If I carry a sack of feed: "This has to be good for me." I can't just stand there and let everything I've worked for go to waste, sit and let the animals lie in their own manure, uncared for, let them starve and die. I can't do that. I can't just let my meadows go to waste. I can't sit there and watch the weeds take over and do nothing. That's not the way I am. I'd rather die. I don't want to be different from the way I am. I don't want to be a different person just to stay alive. If the person I am dies, then I die.—"It's Russian roulette," the voice says. "Every time you climb a ladder or pick up a bag of feed or a bucket of manure, it can be the last." *(Pause.)* I can die. *(Snapping her fingers.)* Just like that.—Next time I run after a sheep. *(Snaps her fingers.)* Like that! *(Standing.)* I can't afford to pay someone to take care of things. *(Showing TRESSA the palms of her hands.)* Look at my hands.

TRESSA takes her hands affectionately.

PAULA: Pete wants to help. He has gone into debt for me. But he can't borrow anymore. He's lost his credit. He's done all he can to help … I can't ask him to do anymore. He humiliates himself for me. They won't lend him anymore money. I can't bear it. You'd think I'd make enough money selling the milk and the wool and the eggs. But I don't. I don't know how to make it work. It costs more to feed the animals than what I can earn from them. I owe that money to Peter. I want to pay him back. He says not to be silly, that he's my husband, and besides, he is my partner. But that's not so. He's gone into it just to help me. He's never understood why I do it—keep my hands in the dirt all day long. I don't want to ask him for money, and I still do it. I ask him for more money. It's a loan. I always say it's a loan. I've never looked kindly on people who can't take care of themselves and their obsessions or their vices; people who make excuses for themselves and make others pay their bills. That's what I'm doing. I know I should sell the animals and most of the land. But I can't. I'm like a drug addict who will do anything to satisfy her vice. I've lost my faith, my honor, my sense of pride. I still have them though ... *(As if seeing them.)* I still have them ... running in my meadow. *(She looks at her hands.)* I do the work because I have to. Because I can't afford to get help. If I didn't, I would have to watch them starve to death. Do you think I could sit there and watch them die in a swamp of manure? I couldn't. I would die first. I couldn't stand seeing them suffer.

TRESSA: *(Saddened.)* ... Oh, Paula.

PAULA: ... Oh, Paula ... *(Standing and crossing to the right of the bench and sitting.)* Oh, Paula.—Don't worry. Don't worry. It doesn't matter. My life is over.—There's nothing to worry about.

TRESSA: Are you crazy? Your life is over?

PAULA: It is. Whether I die or not. I'm serious. From here on it's downhill. A downhill ride. *(She somersaults off the bench down center and remains seated.)* I know my life is over. So my problems are over. *(She sits on the floor.)*

TRESSA: Oh, Paula ...

PAULA: They are. I have suffered disappointment after disappointment, humiliation after humiliation. And I've survived it. So I've nothing to worry about.

TRESSA: Oh, Paula ...

PAULA: *(Interrupting.)* Don't say anything. Forget everything I said. I don't want to depress you.—What are you doing tonight?

TRESSA: I work tonight. What are you doing this afternoon?

PAULA: I'm going out.

TRESSA: *(Walking to PAULA.)* Doing what?

PAULA: I have a couple of things to do in town. Which I won't do till this afternoon, because I'm going back to bed. *(Kissing TRESSA.)* Goodnight. *(Walking up to the bench.)* I'm free for dinner. You want to have dinner? Then I'm going to a party, which you're welcome to come to. Tomorrow I go home bright and early.

As they speak, PAULA fixes the covers on the bench. TRESSA goes to table 2 and continues applying the cream.

TRESSA: When do you think you'll be back?

PAULA: About four, I guess. At what time are you going to work?

TRESSA: Six. Six to midnight.

PAULA: I guess you can't go to the party unless you want to go after work.

TRESSA: I can't see people after work. I have to unwind. If I'm up when you get back, we can have a drink. If we don't see each other tonight, wake me up tomorrow before you leave. Say goodbye.

PAULA: I will. *(Turns to look at TRESSA.)* What is that you're putting on your face?

TRESSA: Cream.

PAULA walks to TRESSA and looks at her face.

PAULA: Hmm.—What does it do?

TRESSA: I like … the way it feels on my skin.

PAULA: It's white?

TRESSA: Yes.

PAULA: It looks nice.

TRESSA: It goes with my pajamas.

PAULA: Yes, it does.

TRESSA: It makes me feel calm to wear this. It soothes me. When I wear this I feel smooth, calm … People dress in a certain way to feel in a certain way. It's natural for me to dress this way. I feel whole. It soothes me.

PAULA: And if you're not dressed like this?

TRESSA: I feel … clumsy.

PAULA: Clumsy?—You're not clumsy.

TRESSA: Maybe I'm not. But I feel clumsy.

PAULA: I think you're very lovely.

TRESSA: I thank you.—I think I'm a cross-dresser.

PAULA: How's that?

TRESSA: Yes.

PAULA: Could you explain that to me?

TRESSA: I don't think I can.... When I dress like this, I feel I'm a man.—I feel I am an Asian man. Thoroughly an Asian man. My heart, my groin, my head, my tongue, my hands, I like to dress like this. I like the way it feels on my body. I like looking at my face in the mirror when I have my yellow face, my oblique eyes. I like the way my voice sounds, the way these clothes make me think. I like my Oriental face. My feet. I feel calm like this. Calm. I'd dress as a Western man to go to a party. To fool around. But when I dress like this I'm not fooling around.

PAULA: Seeing you like this makes me feel I'm with a man ... a lovely man ... How exotic ...

The phone rings. PAULA offers her hand to TRESSA. They do a very quick minuet kind of walk to the timing of the telephone rings. PAULA picks up the receiver and hands it to TRESSA.

TRESSA: Hello ... *(She listens and smiles. She looks at PAULA and mouths the word "Jack." PAULA nods. They both smile with glee.)* Yeah ... *(Pause.)* Yeah ... *(Pause; then TRESSA laughs.)* Oh ... *(Pause; then, in surprise and amusement.)* Oh ... *(Pause; then, in surprise and amusement.)* Oh my God.— Yeah. Yeah. Okay. Right. Yeah-yeah, I know. Fine-fine. Okay. *(Laughs.)* Okay. *(She hangs up the receiver. She laughs again.)* That was Jack. *(She starts down the stairs.)* He's around the corner.

PAULA: Oh boy.

TRESSA: Yes. He's funny.

PAULA: He's a funny guy.

There is the sound of a large door rolling on metal wheels. And the door hitting the wall. PAULA takes a dress and a pair of shoes from behind the screen, examines the dress, starts coming down the left plank and into the bathroom. She reenters and walks up the left plank and behind the screen. She reappears with more clothes and goes into the bathroom. Then she enters and goes up the left plank. TRESSA comes up the steps. She is pensive. She stops center. PAULA turns to her.

PAULA: What's the matter?

TRESSA: Jack is in bad shape. He believes he's ill, but he's not.

PAULA: What do you mean?

TRESSA: He thinks he has AIDS. His friend is very sick. He has AIDS. But Jack doesn't. He's obsessed with it. He tests negative. But he doesn't trust the test. He's sure he's HIV-positive and that he has been for years. The slightest bruise or sore makes him think that it's the start of AIDS. He keeps getting tested. And it keeps coming out negative. *(She walks down right.)* I think he'd be relieved if he tested positive. He's like a paranoid who feels relieved if someone is actually following him. He'd say, "See, I was right. I'm being followed." I can't help him. I can't convince him he doesn't have AIDS. He just thinks the tests are not accurate. On the surface he seems all right, but he's tormented. Obsessed. Sometimes he frightens me. He hallucinates. It will kill him. In the end it will kill him.

The downstairs door is heard opening.

JACK: *(Offstage.)* Hello. *(Pause.)* Anybody home?

PAULA takes her clothes to the bathroom. TRESSA goes to the railing.

TRESSA: Here.

PAULA reenters.

JACK: Cover your eyes.

They cover their eyes. JACK comes upstairs. He wears a false mustache, glasses, a nose, and a gold tooth. He wears a leather jacket and blue jeans.

JACK: Taraaaa … ! ! !

They uncover their eyes.

JACK: Hi girls!

PAULA and TRESSA: Jack … ! ! !

PAULA jumps on JACK and wraps her legs around him. She takes off his costume glasses, nose, and mustache.

PAULA: How wonderful to see you. *(Touches his face, kisses it, kisses his hand.)* How wonderful to be with you. *(Touches his face again.)* Let me see you.

He gives her a big smile showing the gold tooth.

PAULA: Jack!

JACK: What?

PAULA: *(Pointing to the tooth.)* The tooth.

JACK: It's not real. *(He looks at TRESSA and points to the gold tooth.)* Chocolate wrap. How good to see you.

PAULA: It was you!

JACK: What?

PAULA: José Luis.

JACK: Me—José Luis. You—Conchita. *(He laughs.)* You're crazy.

They laugh.

PAULA: *(Taking him by the arm to the left.)* Come with me.

JACK: Where are you taking me?

PAULA: You'll see.

JACK: She has something up her sleeve.

PAULA: I have something up my sleeve.

JACK: What is it?

They exit left.

PAULA: Close your eyes.

JACK: They are closed.

Pause.

TRESSA: Watch it! One more step. *(Pause.)* Turn around.

JACK: Can I open my eyes?

TRESSA: Not yet. *(Pause.)*

JACK: It's a coat!!

TRESSA: Don't look yet!!

JACK: It's a coat! It's a coat! It's a coat! *(He enters wearing a man's nine-teenth-century frock coat, jumping.)* Paula look! It's a coat! It's a coat! Oh! Oh! *(He gets his briefcase from the landing.)* I brought my new play. *(He sits on the bench and opens the briefcase.)* Let's read it. *(Improvising music that vibrates as the birth of a miracle, he slowly brings his hands inside the briefcase and takes out two copies of a play. Holding a copy of the play in each hand, he extends one to TRESSA and one to PAULA.)*

PAULA: *(Gently.)* I'm not up yet.

JACK: *(Disappointed.)* Oh.

PAULA: I haven't washed my face.

JACK: *(Pouting.)* ... You don't have to wash your face ...

PAULA: ... I was on my way to wash up ...

JACK: *(Hugging the scripts to his chest and pouting.)* ... I thought you'd want to read it ...

PAULA: I have to brush my teeth ...

JACK sighs.

PAULA: I won't take long.

JACK: ... Please, don't take long.

PAULA: *(Sweetly.)* I won't. I don't have that many teeth.

JACK: *(Pouting.)* Okay, but don't take long.

PAULA: I won't.

PAULA exits left. JACK throws himself on the floor and has a pouting tantrum. He bangs on the floor with fists and feet.

JACK: She doesn't want to read it ... She doesn't want to read it. *(Toward the bathroom.)* You don't want to read it! *(To the heavens.)* No one wants to read my play! No one wants to read my play! No one wants to read my play! *(He lies on his stomach and bangs his fists on the floor. As he walks to the bathroom.)* How long are you going to take? *(He goes into the bathroom.)* Please, don't take long.

PAULA: *(Amused.)*: Jack ... !

JACK: Five minutes? Three minutes? *(Silence.)* Half an hour?

PAULA: Jack ...

JACK: Ten ... minutes?

PAULA: Go away, Jack.

He enters and goes to TRESSA.

JACK: Would you read it?

TRESSA takes the script and starts to read. JACK sits on the floor to watch her read.

JACK: Paula, Tressa's reading it.

He looks at TRESSA *for signs. He walks away, turns to look at her from a different angle, circles her, lies down with his head propped on his hand. She smiles.*

JACK: Paula, she's smiling.

TRESSA *is still reading. He watches her. She laughs. He contracts with a tremor of pleasure. He watches a while longer. She smiles again, then laughs.*

JACK: Paula, she's laughing!

PAULA: Good.

A moment passes. TRESSA *turns the page. She reads.*

JACK: Paula, she's still reading. It must be good.

PAULA: Is it good, Tressa?

TRESSA: Uh-huh.

PAULA: Can you tell yet?

TRESSA: It's good.

PAULA: What is it about?

TRESSA: Compote.

PAULA: Compost?

TRESSA: Compote, Paula!

PAULA: Is it good?

TRESSA: Yeah. *(To* JACK.*)* When did you write this?

JACK: *(Professional.)* It's just a first draft. It's not there yet. I just started it. *(Stands and paces, doing important-person gestures.)* The premise. A man and a woman. He, from the city. She, from a farm, Vermont. The conflict between urban and rural life. Two different cultures. That is the premise. *(Pause.)* It has saved my life. It has made me calm down, be still. I don't spend nights roaming around the city anymore.

TRESSA: You weren't here last night?

JACK: No. Why?

TRESSA: The gold tooth.

JACK: *(Taking out the gold foil.)* Just foil.

TRESSA: Paula dreamt you came in with a gold tooth.

JACK: She did? Hmm. Smart. *(Pointing to his own head.)* She's smart. *(Pointing to where PAULA is.)* Smart girl. *(Speaking out to PAULA.)* Paula.

PAULA: What?

JACK: You dreamt about my tooth.

PAULA: That's right. *(She enters. She wears a smart business suit, high heels, and makeup.)*

JACK: God, Paula, you look great!

PAULA poses.

JACK: Where are you going?

PAULA: I'm doing a few errands.

JACK: You have a date?

PAULA: … No, I don't have a date.

JACK: Tell Jack.

PAULA: *(Dropping the pose.)* I'm seeing a man about a job.

JACK: A man?

PAULA: A job.

JACK: A job? In town?

PAULA: No, not in town.

JACK: Oh, I thought you'd stay in town.

PAULA: Not in town. Freelance. From home.

JACK: What's the job?

PAULA: Research.

JACK: On what?

PAULA: Husbandry.

JACK: That's right up your alley.

PAULA: Yeap.

JACK: For whom?

PAULA: A conservancy magazine.

JACK: Ah! I hope you get it.

PAULA: Have my fingers crossed.

JACK: Cross mine too.

PAULA: I'll also be meeting a man about a loan.

JACK: Hmm. What man?

PAULA: A man at a bank. I owe money.

JACK: Hmm. The farm?

PAULA *nods.*

JACK: Hope you get it.

PAULA: Yeah.

JACK: You should get all the money you need.

PAULA: I sure should.

JACK: How could they refuse you?

PAULA: They couldn't.

JACK: Of course they couldn't.

PAULA: I'm also going to see Dr. Eckland.

JACK: ... Eckland ...

PAULA: Cardiologist.

JACK: Oh?

PAULA: Uh-huh.

JACK: You?

PAULA: Yeap.

JACK: Since when?

PAULA: A while. He's going to do some tests.

JACK: That's a bunch of things you're doing.

PAULA: That's right. You see why I have to look sharp.

JACK: That's right.

PAULA: *(Laughs.)* Have to impress those machines.

JACK: It's an important day.

PAULA: Yeap. Loaded.

JACK: I hope you score.

PAULA: Uh-huh.—Pray for me. *(To TRESSA.)* Pray for me.

TRESSA: With all my heart.

PAULA: Jack.—What made you put on that gold tooth and nose and mustache?

JACK: I don't know ... Nothing.

PAULA: When you came in like that, I was confused.

JACK: Why?

PAULA: Last night I dreamt of a man who came in here looking just like that.

JACK: You did?

PAULA: Yes. Did you know that?

JACK: No. I just thought it was funny.

PAULA: Why is that funny?

JACK: *(Shrugs.)* I got it at a funny trick store.

PAULA: *(Starting to go toward the bathroom.)* Take it back. Tell them nobody found it funny. Get a refund.

JACK: *(Laughs.)* How's Pete?

PAULA: Pete's fine.

JACK: How're the kids?

PAULA: Kids? They're taller than Pete.

JACK: How's that possible?

PAULA: *(From the bathroom.)* It's been three years. You haven't been up in three years, Jack.

JACK: Three years?

PAULA: *(Offstage.)* Yep.

JACK: You couldn't be right.

PAULA: *(Offstage.)*: That's what it is. Three years. Last time you came up was three years ago, it was spring.

JACK: Is that right?

PAULA: *(Offstage.)* Yeah. That's the last time you came up. Three years ago.

JACK: Three years ...

PAULA: *(Offstage.)* That's right.

JACK: *(Going to* TRESSA.*)* Does that sound right to you?

TRESSA: That sounds right. That's when I got the red quilt.

JACK: The red quilt ... Three years since the red quilt. Can't believe it. How time passes. *(Sits and leans his head on his hands.)* I can't believe it. Oh my God. Oh my God. *(He looks up. His eyes are full of tears. He walks right and kneels next to* TRESSA.*)* Oh my God. Oh my God ... How life slips through your fingers.

TRESSA *extends her arms to* JACK.

TRESSA: *(Strokes his head.)* It does. It does. *(Pause.)* What's wrong, my sweet?

JACK: ... I'm fine ... I'm fine. How time passes ... How time passes ...

TRESSA *strokes his head.*

TRESSA: Are you working?

JACK: ... Here and there ...

TRESSA: What are you doing?

JACK: ASM.

TRESSA: ASM?

JACK: Associate Sado-Masochist. *(Short pause.)* Assistant Stage Manager. Backstage work.

PAULA: *(From the bathroom.)* Oops. What happened? The light went out. It must be the bulb.

JACK: I'll get it. *(Goes to the bathroom.)*

PAULA: *(Offstage.)* It's dark here.

JACK: *(Offstage.)* I'll be right back.

JACK enters, gets a bulb from the cabinet, and returns to the bathroom.

JACK: *(Offstage.)* Where are you?

PAULA: Here.

JACK: Hold this. Do you have a match?

PAULA: No, Jack. I don't have a match.

JACK: Ouch! It's hot.

PAULA: Wait till it cools.

JACK: You mean stand here and wait till it cools?

PAULA: Well, why not?

They laugh.

JACK: You're silly.

PAULA: Here's something.

JACK: What?

PAULA: A washcloth.

JACK: It's wet!

PAULA: Yeah. Let me get something else. *(Short pause.)* Here's a towel. It's dry.

JACK: Okay. *(Short pause.)* Where's the bulb? It was here a moment ago.

PAULA: Give me your hand.

JACK: Here's my hand. Where's yours?

They laugh.

JACK: Here it is. I have it.—Okay. *(Short pause.)* Hold this.

PAULA: Is it still hot?

JACK: Hold it with the towel. *(Short pause.)* Where's the other bulb? Where did I put the other bulb? Here it is.—Okay. *(Pause. Then the light goes on.)*

PAULA: Thank you.

JACK: You're welcome. *(Jack appears at the door. He stands for a while. He is downcast.)* Joey died.

TRESSA: ... Oh!

JACK walks down and sits.

JACK: That's why I haven't been around.—I've been a mess. I fell apart. But I wrote this. It's not great, but I like it. I like the characters. They are sweet. It kept me from going away.

PAULA enters. She stays in the back.

JACK: I couldn't stand thinking that he was dead. That I would never see him again. I couldn't sleep. I kept wandering and wandering through the streets ... the places we used to go to. But that was too painful, remembering him. Then I went to places I had never been to. But then I got scared because, when I had no memories of him, I felt desperate. But I couldn't go home, because everything there reminded me of him. I saw him everywhere. I couldn't sleep. I saw him sitting in every chair. I saw him in every corner. In the tub, by the sink, on the toilet. On the bed, under the sheets. On top of the covers. I couldn't rest. I couldn't eat. Then I thought I was going to die. Then I wrote this. *(To PAULA.)* You met him ... He was my love ... He died. He was the sweetest person on earth. That's why I loved him. He was good. Like you. You're good. That's why I love you. You're good. *(To TRESSA.)* I'm not good. I don't know how to be good. I never had that feeling in my heart. Never. I'm just clever, that's all. I laugh at things. I'm not good inside. The most tender I can be is when I'm witty. That's the best I can be. I don't know how to be good. I love goodness, though. I wish I could be good. It's peaceful. Isn't it, ... being good? When I'm witty, I feel close to being good, but it's not the same. I feel a little tender when I'm witty. But it's not the same. Joey was good. You could see it in his face, in his body. There was no poison in them. His body was like a baby's. No nerves. No tendons. *(To PAULA.)* Like you. *(To*

Tressa.) You're good. *(To Paula.)* You're good. *(To both.)* That's why I love you. You and he are the only persons I've loved. And I killed him.

Jack is now crying. Tressa goes to him.

JACK: *(Very intensely.)*
It was I who killed him.
It was I who killed him.
I gave him AIDS.
It was I who gave him AIDS.
I killed him. I killed him.

TRESSA:
No, Jack. You didn't. You don't have AIDS. You're not contagious. You're not HIV positive. You're negative.

Jack walks left and sits at the table.

JACK: His family is being terrible. They didn't want me to see him when he was dying. They didn't want me to go to the funeral. They took all his things. Things I had given him. I didn't want any of it. I just wanted the fur coat that used to be mine, and I didn't want anymore, and I'd given it to him because he loved it. That's the only reason I wanted it, because he loved it. He loved to touch it. He loved to lie in bed wearing nothing but the coat. He loved the way it felt on his body. And that's why I wanted it. Because having that coat would make me feel that I still had him. They thought I wanted it because it was valuable. It was an old coat. I wanted to get naked and wear it and feel him.

Jack lowers his head slowly. Tressa and Paula look at him in silence awhile. Paula goes to him. She kisses his forehead.

PAULA: Remember Shangri-la … ? Remember Shangri-la?

Jack nods.

PAULA: What did the High Lama say to Conway?

JACK: *(Tearful. He quotes words from* Lost Horizon.*)* "The storm, this storm you talked of … "

Paula: "I believe you will live through the storm, my child. You will still live through the long age of desolation" …

Jack joins her.

PAULA and JACK: … "growing older and wiser and more patient."

Tressa joins them.

PAULA, JACK, and TRESSA: "You will conserve the fragrance of our history hidden behind the valley of Shangri-la. You will conserve the fragrance of our history hidden behind the valley of Shangri-la."

Short pause.

PAULA: … Let's read your play.

JACK: … Yes.

They take the scripts, walk to the upstage area. PAULA and TRESSA sit at each end of the bench. JACK sits on the chair left. "Banks of the Ohio" from Music of the Ozarks [National Geographic Society] plays.

JACK: *"A one-room cottage on a farm in Vermont. The cottage is impeccably clean. Wilma and Eric sit at the table. Eric wears a suit. Wilma wears a housedress."*

ERIC: *(Read by one of the women with a heavy German accent.)* This is a very good compote.

WILMA: *(Read by the other woman with a heavy German accent.)* Yah. It is very good compote. And very good bread. I make the bread myself sometimes. This one I didn't make, but it is made the same way as the bread I make. And this butter is the best. It couldn't be better, because it's made with fresh milk of cows that put out very creamy milk that is tasty, because milk can have a bland taste. Here is salt. You can put in it salt. Taste it. You look hungry. You want milk. Milk tastes good with bread. It just came out of the cow. It's still warm from the udder.

ERIC: The udder what?

WILMA: The udder from the cow.—Dunk the bread. If you dunk the bread in the milk, it gets damp with the milk and it tastes better.

They drink.

ERIC and WILMA: Aha!

WILMA: My hand is damp. *(She puts her hand on ERIC's cheek. Pause.)* See? I will dry it on my apron because it is damp. *(She dries her hand and puts it on his cheek again. Pause.)* See? *(She takes the hand away.)* Now it is dry. It is good to keep your hand dry.—Eat, this is the best. Do you know cows better than these ones?

ERIC: I don't know other cows.

WILMA: I thought you knew other cows.

ERIC: No.

WILMA: It is a pity. Are you not ashamed?

ERIC: I am not ashamed. In the city there are no cows. In the city it is not a pity not to know a cow.

WILMA: Not?

ERIC: No. A cow is large. There is no place to keep a cow in house in the city. And also a lot of people live in apartment. And apartment is smaller than house.

WILMA: Apartment is smaller than house?

ERIC: Of course. Some people have yard and garden. But they don't want to keep a cow in garden.

WILMA: Why not?

ERIC: Why not?

WILMA: Yes. Why not?

ERIC: To keep a cow in garden?

WILMA: Why not?

ERIC: Oh.—One, the cow would trample the grass and eat it. Do cows eat flowers?

WILMA: Of course cows eat flowers.

ERIC: Two.—The cow would eat the flowers. Do cows moo?

WILMA looks at ERIC.

WILMA: *(Indignant and condescending.)* Do cows moo? Of course cows moo.

ERIC: Well, the cow will moo then.

WILMA: Cows have to moo. Do you want a cow not to moo? Do you want a cow to say, "I would like to be milked now, please milk me now."—Is that what you want the cow to do?

ERIC: Do cows moo at night?

WILMA: No, cows do not moo at night.

ERIC: At what time do they moo?

WILMA: When did the cow go to sleep?

ERIC: I don't know when the cow went to sleep.

WILMA: She moos because she needs milking.

ERIC: She needs milking?

WILMA: Of course.

ERIC: Why?

WILMA: Because the milk fills the udders, and it hurts the udders.

ERIC: What udder?

WILMA: The udder of the cow. If they are milked at six they will moo at six.

ERIC: Like nurses.

WILMA: What?

ERIC: Yah. Six would be too early. A cow mooing at six would wake up everyone.

WILMA: Six is good time to wake up.

ERIC: In the city people get angry to be wakened at six by a cow.

WILMA: I don't see how they could drink fresh *milken* then.

ERIC: In the city milk is delivered from the country in bottles every day.

WILMA: If it is delivered from the country, and the bottles make a tinkle sound, it is not fresh then. It is old milk. It is not like the milk in that glass. Don't drink the milk in the bottle. It is not fresh. Drink this. It is fresh.

They drink some milk, lick their lips, smack their lips, and put their glasses down.

WILMA: Yah!

The lights fade to suggest a passage of time. As country music ["Down in the Arkansas," Music of the Ozarks, National Geographic Society] plays, JACK does a cowboy two-step moving to the downstage area.

JACK: "Act two. A year later. Spring approaches. WILMA wears a housedress. ERIC wears a straw hat and pair of overalls."

JACK does a turn doing the two-step and lies down on the downstage bench facing the readers. The music ends.

ERIC: I'm going to buy two cows, or one cow and six goats, or ten pigs and some hens. Or not buy cows, and build a shed, and buy land, or put money in the bank.

WILMA: Eric, my husband, you work too hard. You want to work all the time?—Put some fish in the pond and we can go fishing on Sundays.

ERIC: Good Wilma. I am so glad I have you for a wife. I am happy because you are my wife, Wilma, my wife.

Wilma: I am happy, Eric, my husband. Put fish in the pond and we can go fishing on Sundays.

ERIC: Ah, yah. I am glad I married you, Wilma. You make life a paradise.

WILMA: Ahh, Eric, my husband. I am glad.

They hold hands.

WILMA and ERIC: Yaaaaah!

PAULA and TRESSA: *(Applauding.)* Very good, Jack! Very good, Jack!

"Angel Band" from Music of the Ozarks [National Geographic Society] starts playing softly. PAULA and TRESSA go to each side of JACK. He goes toward the plank, faces them, and bows.

PAULA: That is so beautiful, Jack.

JACK: I thank you.

TRESSA: It is so dear.

JACK: *(Starting to walk backwards down the plank.)* Thank you.

TRESSA: Oh, Jack, I want to cry.

JACK: Cry?

PAULA: I cried, Jack.

JACK walks toward center as TRESSA and PAULA walk down the plank.

TRESSA: It is so sweet.

JACK is shyly thrilled and excited. He drops to the floor. They run to him and drop on each side of him and hug him.

JACK: *(Opening his arms and speaking religiously.)* To Joey!

TRESSA and PAULA: To Joey!

PAULA: May your heart live!

JACK: May your heart live!

TRESSA: … May your heart live …

"Icy Blue Heart," by John Hiatt, plays. JACK's hands go up in the air, then to his mouth. He blows a kiss as he throws his hands up.

JACK: Now we celebrate.

TRESSA and PAULA: We celebrate.

The volume of music goes up. They dance through the following. Jack goes to the stairs and goes down a few steps. He throws a tablecloth and napkins over the railing. TRESSA catches the tablecloth and lays it on the table. PAULA catches the napkins. TRESSA goes to the kitchen and gets glasses, a bowl of fruit, a paring knife, and a bell. JACK comes up with a paper bag, a bakery box, and a bottle of wine. They set the table. He opens the bottle. PAULA opens the box and takes out croissants, then takes out cheese from the paper bag. They sit around the table, raise their napkins, shake them, and place them on their laps in time with the music.

JACK: *(Raising his glass.)* Breakfast!

TRESSA sounds the bell. TRESSA and PAULA raise their glasses and toast with JACK.

TRESSA, PAULA, and JACK: Breakfast!

They drink and eat.

TRESSA: *(Toasting.)* May Art live!

ALL: *(Toasting.)* May Art live!

They drink and eat. The music begins to fade.

PAULA: *(Toasting.)* May Theatre live!

ALL: *(Toasting.)* May Theatre live!

They drink and eat.

JACK: *(Toasting.)* May Poetry live!

ALL: *(Toasting.)* May Poetry live!

PAULA *walks around the table.*

PAULA: What would you give up to be the greatest artist in the world? Would you give up your youth? … Tressa?

TRESSA: I would. How much would I have to give up?

PAULA: Seven years.

TRESSA *thinks.*

TRESSA: … Seven years …

PAULA: See? We're not interested in art. We're only interested in seduction. *(Continues walking around the table.)* When we're young, we pretend we want to be artists. But all we're interested in is seduction. We want the world to have a crush on us. We want to be irresistible.

JACK *and* TRESSA *at the same time mumble the following:*

JACK: Not me. I never felt that.

TRESSA: That's not so. Art comes first.

PAULA: Would you give up your youthful good looks to be the greatest artists in the world?

JACK and TRESSA: Yeah … Yeah …

PAULA: Look like Quasimodo?

JACK *and* TRESSA *applaud.* PAULA *leans on* JACK *with her arms around him.*

Jack:	Tressa:
Well no. Not that. You're right. I wouldn't.	No, not like Quasimodo. That's true. I wouldn't.

TRESSA: Yet it doesn't matter. If you're a good artist, you will be loved no matter what.

JACK: I wouldn't say no matter what.

TRESSA: Ugly artists get loved more than other ugly people.

JACK: Ugly rich people get loved more than ugly artists.

TRESSA: True, but next to ugly rich people I think it's ugly artists.

JACK: Yeap.

PAULA: Yeah.

TRESSA: To ugly artists.

PAULA and JACK: To ugly artists.

TRESSA: *(Peeling an apple.)* My mother loved people for their beauty, and yet she loved my father because he was an artist. He wasn't good-looking. And yet she loved him.—Why? Because he was an artist.—Even if she only loved people for their beauty, she fell in love with him because he was an artist. He didn't look like Quasimodo, but he wasn't the prettiest thing on earth. Yet she loved him.—She once loved a girl because she was beautiful. She told me she wanted the girl to love her, but she didn't. My father loved my mother because she was beautiful. He, too, loved people for their beauty. He loved my brother because he was beautiful, and he liked to paint him. He didn't like me because I wasn't beautiful.

JACK: PAULA:
You weren't beautiful?   What do you mean you were not beautiful?

TRESSA: *(Ignoring their objections.)* He painted my brother all the time and not me. My mother wanted me to like a girl who lived nearby just because she was beautiful. I didn't like that girl, and I told her I didn't love people just because they were beautiful, and I didn't like her. But she said, "You should still like her. Because she's beautiful." I didn't like her, and that was that. *(Going to the kitchen. To Jack.)* She didn't like you because you weren't beautiful.

JACK: I wasn't beautiful?

PAULA goes to the bench and sits as TRESSA enters.

TRESSA: She said you weren't. My brother said that you were cute because you looked like me. And she said you didn't.

JACK: I look like you?

TRESSA: Yes. That's the reason why I liked you. I didn't like girls except for you.

JACK: Me? *(Laughs.)*

TRESSA: *(Reaching toward PAULA.)* Since then I've never liked a girl except for Paula, who is my love. Whom I have loved for years and who won't have me. Because she loves Jack. And won't have me. Because she only has eyes for Jack.

JACK: *(Sitting to the left of PAULA and hugging her.)* Me, too. My eyes are for

Paula, my Paula. I only have eyes for you. You should love me and not mean Huang.

PAULA: Huang?

JACK: Yes, that person there is Huang.

PAULA: Paula loves you. She loves you and she always will. Even after death will she love you.

JACK: Paula will not die. She will live forever to love Jack.

TRESSA: *(Standing.)* ... Paula's not well, Jack.

Pause.

PAULA: I'm fine. *(She flexes her muscles.)* I'm fine. I had heart palpitations like fibrillations. *(Pinching JACK's cheek.)* My heart beat so fast I thought it would burst. Peter prepared an injection that makes the heart relax, and I was okay. Had this continued for one more minute I would have died. But I didn't.

JACK: So many people are ill ... so many people ... Everyone is ill. One day every single person will be ill ... old illnesses ... new illnesses ... old symptoms ... new symptoms ... old treatments ... new treatments ... *(Starting to clear the table. In the course of the speech, JACK takes everything on the table to the kitchen.)* Everything in our minds will be illness, the ill, the dying. All art will be about illness. All plays will be about illness. And the ill. The characters will be defined by their illness. It is the characters' illnesses that will determine the plot. Instead of the ingénue, the romantic lead, the friend, the villain, the characters will be defined by their illnesses: the cancer victim, the AIDS victim, the tubercular, the diabetic. The person poisoned by industrial chemicals, in the air, in food. The central issue of the plots will be the development of the illness: the first notice of the symptoms, the first visit to the doctor, the relationship with the doctors, with other patients, with family, with one's own body, with side effects, how one copes. Treatment will be an integral part of the plot.—The plots will be whether to save one patient or the other: possibility of blackmail, bribes in exchange for special treatment, relationships with the attending doctor: attachment, hatred, jealousy toward other patients. Or bank robberies to pay for medical care. The murder mysteries will be: Patients of a renowned doctor are murdered. The doctor is suspected, but the murderer is a patient who is waiting his turn for an operation, and he may die before the doctor can get to him, so he kills all patients who are scheduled before him. The serial murders will be: The patient kills everyone who has the same disease as him so he can have his choice of physician. After a while, plays will be more subtle. Each character will suffer a different illness. The illness won't be mentioned, but the audience will be able to identify it by the way the characters walk, the way they stand, the way they breathe. Does his hand go up to a certain part of the body? His side, his neck? Does he need to catch his breath? The best actors will be the ones who can reproduce the particular breathing for each illness. We'll notice the way the character enters, the way they sit, the way they kiss. We'll notice the way they avoid contact with each other. The audience will also be able to identify the illness by the little pills the characters bring to their mouths. Is it the one with the yellow stripe, or the royal blue stripe? The bottle with the blue label? What is the gravity of the illness? Is the character taking one, two, or more pills at a time? How frequently? The leading characters will have the illness most common among theatregoers. Since theatregoers prefer to have plays written about them. Plays will be funded by pharmaceutical laboratories.

There is a pause.

PAULA: *(Standing.)* Well ... it's time for me to go.

JACK: *(Distressed.)* Are you going to the doctor now?

PAULA: Don't worry. We're all a part of it ... Not one of us is invulnerable to it. *(Pause.)* Where is my briefcase? *(She looks for it and exits left. She reenters with the briefcase.)* Here it is. Okay, I'll be back. *(She goes to the landing and starts down.)*

JACK: *(Starting to go down.)* I'll walk you down.

PAULA: Heavens, I'm not an invalid.

JACK: *(Stopping.)* Of course.

TRESSA: You don't want me to drive you?

PAULA: Heavens, no. I have my car.

She starts down the steps. JACK leans over the railing.

JACK: Give me a kiss.

PAULA gives him a kiss. She continues down.

JACK: Tell them what I think of you.

TRESSA: Tell them to give you all their money.

PAULA: I will.

JACK: You just tell them that. And tell them to give you that job.

PAULA: Okay.

TRESSA: And tell the doctor there's nothing wrong with you.

PAULA: I will.—Thanks, you all. See you later.

TRESSA: Good luck.

PAULA: Thank you.

JACK: Don't take any wooden nickels.

PAULA laughs.

PAULA: I won't.

TRESSA: Are you going to be back for dinner?

PAULA: I think so.

JACK: I'm bringing Chinese.

The lights begin to fade.

PAULA: Good. I'll be here, then.

TRESSA: We're eating early. I have to be at work at six.

PAULA: At what time should I be back?

TRESSA: Four-thirty will be good.

PAULA: Okay.

JACK: … Goodbye …

PAULA: Goodbye.

A moment passes.

JACK: … Goodbye …

A moment passes.

JACK: … Goodbye …

There is the sound of the door closing. JACK turns to face front. He looks gloomy. There is a pause.

JACK: Three years since I last saw her …

The lights fade to black.

★ ACT TWO

JACK and TRESSA perform scenes from D. W. Griffith's Broken Blossoms *while silent-movie organ music plays. JACK performs Lillian Gish's part, the GIRL, and wears the loose frock of a waif. TRESSA performs Richard Barthelmess's part, HUANG, and wears a Chinese box jacket and pants. They first walk in opposite directions around the stage, reenacting the scene where the GIRL has been beaten by her father and wanders the streets to finally faint on the floor of HUANG's shop (upstage). HUANG takes her up to his room (downstage) and dresses her in an embroidered silk gown, lowers her to his bed, and puts makeup on her face and a decorative crown of flowers on her head. She falls asleep as he exits. A moment later, turbulent music is heard. An invisible Father enters. The GIRL is terrified. The Father shakes her and throws her on the floor, grabs her by the arm, and takes her home. There he beats her unconscious and leaves. HUANG enters to find the GIRL dying. He holds her in his arms as she dies. They stay motionless for a while. PAULA comes up the stairs and watches the last minutes of their act. PAULA walks to them. She looks at them and touches JACK's face and the ornaments on his face. She touches TRESSA's face. She walks around the front, goes to the kitchen, and reenters with a flan mold on a plate and a spoon. She eats a few mouthfuls of the flan. JACK and TRESSA start to come out of their stillness and walk slowly downstage to PAULA.*

PAULA: When I was little, I had a cousin who was my age. I loved him very much. He was very nice to me. He was my first lover. We did everything. He put his peepee inside me, and I enjoyed it very much. The first time he tried, he wasn't able to put it in very far. But each time after, he put it in a little further, until he came in all the way, which wasn't very far because we were very little. Each time we enjoyed it more. I learned to come with him. But I didn't come each time. And I got very upset when I didn't. He said he didn't mind. He said he liked it when I came, and he liked it when I didn't. I said, "Well, I don't," and he said that he liked to see me desperate and frustrated. And I said, "Why?" And he said, "Because then I know you want something from me." He saw my frustration as desire. Which it was. He was a sweet darling and … And I forgave him. He was eight, and so was I. *(Pause.)* I saw the doctor.—He says it's kind of bad.—He said that if the fibrillations had lasted any longer, I could have died. I asked him, and that's what he said—that it was true. He said that Peter should teach the kids to do an intravenous injection in case it happens when he is not home.—But I don't have too much hope for that. It's difficult to do. So I suppose I would have to do it myself. But how can I give myself an intravenous injection while having that horrible feeling that my heart is coming out of my mouth? I don't know if I can do it. So I suppose I will have to die.

PAULA *leans her head against* JACK's *head, walks around to the bench, and faces them.*

PAULA: You look beautiful together ... I never imagined ... *(Short pause.)* Do you mind that I saw you ... ?

TRESSA *and* JACK *shake their heads.*

PAULA: It's *Broken Blossoms*, isn't it?

JACK: *(Almost in a whisper.)* ... Yes.

Pause.

PAULA: ... Do you mind my asking?

TRESSA: ... No.

PAULA: ... Is this something you do?

JACK: ... Yes.

Pause.

PAULA: ... Are you lovers?

JACK: ... We love each other ... *(Touching their clothes.)* ... And we love this ... It is very satisfying.

PAULA: ... *Broken Blossoms?*

TRESSA: ... Oh yes ...

PAULA: ... Does it satisfy you ... ? I mean ... do you?

TRESSA: ... Oh yes ...

PAULA: Huang ... ? Do you always wear ... ? I mean ... is this a man's outfit?

TRESSA: ... Yes.

PAULA: ... Do you ever wear women's clothes ... when you are with him?

JACK *walks slowly to the upper bench and sits peacefully.*

TRESSA: ... No.

PAULA: ... Why not?

TRESSA: *(After a short pause.)* Once I knew why. *(Short pause.)* It makes him nervous.

PAULA: What does?

TRESSA: I think it does. *(To Jack.)* Does it make you nervous? *(She looks at him.)* Yes, it makes him nervous.

PAULA: What does?

TRESSA: The woman.

PAULA: You're a lovely woman.

JACK: ... She's a lovely man.

TRESSA: I like to wear this ... *(Walking around the left of the bench and turning to them.)* It soothes me. I wear this when he comes.

PAULA: Why is that?

Tressa: He's calm. I like him when he's calm.

PAULA: Do you think he will fall in love with you if you dress like a man?

TRESSA: Yes. He did once ...

PAULA: He did?

TRESSA: Yes.

PAULA: Fall in love with you?

TRESSA: Yes.

PAULA: Did you fall in love with him?

TRESSA: *(Sitting by the foot of the bench.)* Yes.

PAULA: Are you still in love with him?

TRESSA: In love with him ... *(Sitting.)* I am in love with him. Of course I am. I'll always be ... Always, but not in the same way ...

PAULA: I'm glad you're clear about that.

TRESSA: It's very clear.

PAULA: *(Going to her and kissing her on the forehead.)* I love you, Huang.

TRESSA: He did love me—one night.

PAULA: Oh?

TRESSA: We dressed up for a costume party. We left here arm-in-arm.

JACK *stands, walks slowly to the upper bench, sits, and listens peacefully.*

TRESSA: At the party I saw him looking at me lovingly. Then we danced. And we danced some more. And we danced and we danced. He was nervous, and his hands were trembling. We danced very close, and I felt his heart pounding in his chest. It went boom-boom. Boom-boom. Boom-boom. He was sweating, and he looked frightened. He stared away from me as he held me closer and closer. He smiled nervously and he said, "Let's go home." He took me home, and we made love.

PAULA: Jack … ?

TRESSA: Jack.

JACK: Yes I did.

PAULA: When was that?

TRESSA: Many years ago.

PAULA: … Did I know you then?

TRESSA: Yes. *(She laughs.)*

PAULA: What were you wearing?

TRESSA: A tuxedo.

PAULA: A tuxedo. Then what happened?

TRESSA: I didn't see him for a long time.

PAULA: Coward.

TRESSA: Not I. *(Pause.)* He went away. And didn't come back for a long time. Then one day he came. He was quiet, nervous, scared that something would happen. Scared that I would want something to happen. I didn't show my feelings.—Things went back to normal. He started coming to see me again. I noticed that if I wore a dress, he'd be nervous. If I wore pants, he was relaxed. One day I dressed like this. And I felt very calm, and he was very calm. And he came close to me and he said, "Huang." And I said, "Yes." And he held me close and he whispered … *Broken Blossoms?* … And I said, "Yes." He was beautiful, and I felt beautiful, and it was beautiful just the way we were with each other, at peace with each other.

PAULA: Do you still want him?

TRESSA: Once in love, always in love. We're friends, I love him, and he loves me. Like friends. That's the way love is.

PAULA: *(Goes to the table and sits right. To TRESSA.)* Do you want to buy my house? They're going to sell it. Maybe in the future you can ask me to visit.—And maybe I won't be able to visit. I couldn't stand going there and thinking it belongs to anyone else. Even you. Why are they willing to sell it for nothing to anyone but me? Why can't I buy it for nothing the way anyone else can? *(Short pause.)* Are we going to cook, or go out?

TRESSA: Let's get Chinese. Jack, you want to go get some food?

Paula starts walking around TRESSA slowly. She is observing her. Looking at her under a different light.

JACK: … Sure … *(Going behind the screen.)* What do you want?

TRESSA: Mushu pork.

JACK: And you, Paula?

PAULA: Chicken with mushrooms.

JACK: *(To himself, from behind the screen.)* Moo goo gai pan.

PAULA: *(To TRESSA.)*: Are you coming to the party?

TRESSA: Tonight?

PAULA: Yes.

TRESSA: I have to work.

PAULA: After work.

TRESSA: No … I'll be tired then.

JACK comes out from behind the screen. He is wearing jeans and a leather jacket.

JACK: You want rice?

PAULA: Fried rice.

TRESSA: Steamed rice.

JACK: *(Pointing to each as he repeats their choices.)* Mushu pork. Chicken and mushrooms. Moo goo gai pan. Fried rice. Steamed rice. Steamed rice. *(He starts exiting.)* You want fortune cookies?

TRESSA: Yeah.

PAULA: Sure.

JACK: Yeah.

JACK exits whistling as the lights fade.

It is 2:00 a.m. The lights are dim. JACK's leather jacket is on the back of a chair. There is a light downstairs. JACK's voice is heard from below. He memorizes the backstage work from Everett Quinton's Tale of Two Cities *at The Ridiculous Theatrical Company.*

JACK: Preshow. Open dressing room. Turn on hot water to sink and shower. Set clothes up in dressing room. Check water, cups, Kleenex. Costumes checked *(checklist)*. Turn on water to bathtub. Turn on work and running lights. Drain water barrel. Open prop cabinet. Set up all props. Check winch and track. Check main drape and wig pipe. Patch hole. Set up costumes from closet. Check preset. Set up closet and curtain.

A light is turned on in the bedroom.

JACK: Give deck ready to stage manager. Fix food—Act One. Open main curtain. Show starts—strike window light. Closet opens—knock over closet pile. Door closes—move basket to doorway. Everett sits after phone—ring doorbell. Ding-dong. Cue: "Goddamn it."

TRESSA enters from the bedroom. She watches JACK.

JACK: Knock on door. Door starts to open—run behind set. Basket on dresser—open trap door. Donut handed to baby—toss downstage right. After donut toss—reset closet stuff and Manette stuff.

TRESSA: Jack.

JACK: Hi.

TRESSA: What are you doing?

JACK: I'm going over my backstage running list.

TRESSA: What running list?

JACK: The show I'm stage managing. It's a tough show to run. Ridiculous theatre. Things move too fast. I have to memorize it. Otherwise I won't be able to keep up. Things happen just like this. *(Snapping his fingers repeatedly.)* One after the other. Would you check me on this?

TRESSA: Okay.

JACK: After donut toss—open trap door. You see where that is?

TRESSA: Okay. Yeah. Go ahead.

JACK: After donut toss—reset closet stuff and set Manette stuff. Pross entrance—open trap door. Fork into basket—grab fork and hand off broken fork. After fork taken—close trap door. Cue: "Anything but black bread and death"—ring doorbell. Handoff from Everett—receive wig head from Everett. Door closed—take wig head to closet. Everett into closet—hand white wig to Everett, label up. Everett into closet—tap on closet wall. Everett out of closet—stop tapping. After Manette scene—open trap door. Cue: "Crush him under the wheels"—receive frame and box. Closet opens, Everett into closet—help Everett into coat and swagger stick. Cue: "Feed you with a slingshot"—squirt Everett with water bottle. After squirt—close trap door. During broadcast—receive clothes. TV report— receive TV. Alarm *(Makes alarm sound.)* —set pannier. Cue: "Very good understanding, Mr. Darnay."

TRESSA: "A health, a toast."

JACK: Right! "A health, a toast"—open trap door. Then "Very good understanding, Mr. Darnay"—raise baby in basket. Cue: "Evremonde!!!!!"— raise baby knife, hold three beats, and lower. After knife—close trap door. Cue: "She must not find us together"—help Everett with pannier, basket, and Christmas garland, and start *(Singing.)* "O come all ye faithful." Cue: "God bless you, Sidney"—receive pannier, etc. Cue: "Work comrades all"—hand out red sheet. *(He comes upstairs carrying two blankets, a pillow, the script, and a flashlight and starts making his bed on the downstage bench. He is wearing jeans and a tee shirt.)* Now I have to memorize the second act.

TRESSA: You need some rest.

JACK: *(Lies down and covers himself with the blanket.)* I'll do it tomorrow.

TRESSA kisses him on the cheek and starts left.

TRESSA: Try to get some sleep.

JACK: I will.

TRESSA: Goodnight.

JACK: Goodnight.

TRESSA exits. JACK turns on the flashlight and very quietly memorizes the following:

JACK: Raise baby knife, hold three beats, and lower. After knife—close trap door. Raise baby knife, hold three beats, and lower. After knife—close trap door. Cue: "She must not find us together"—

The lights begin to fade as he starts to doze off and his voice becomes softer.

JACK: Help Everett with pannier, basket, and Christmas garland, and start ... "O come all ye faithful" ...

The lights fade to a very dim level. A few seconds pass.

It is 4:00 a.m. The lights remain the same. JACK is still asleep. The upstage door opens, then closes. PAULA's footsteps are heard below. Something is knocked down.

PAULA: What was that? *(Pause.)* Jack? *(Pause.)* Are you there?

Cans drop and roll downstairs. JACK begins to stir.

PAULA: God! *(Pause.)* What's the matter with this light? *(PAUSE.)* Jack.

Something falls downstairs.

PAULA: Damn it! *(Pause.)* It's dark here.

Something falls downstairs.

PAULA: What's this?

The sound of something being thrown. She starts upstairs.

PAULA: Jack.

JACK: ... What ... ?

PAULA: I hit your car, and I don't know if I damaged it.—I think I did. But it wasn't my fault, and I'm not paying for it.—You were parked in the wrong direction, and that's illegal. If you take me to court you won't collect, because it's illegal to park in the wrong direction. The front of the car doesn't reflect an oncoming car, so if you're coming into it, you can't see it. It was dark, and I didn't see it.—I didn't even see the road. I was drunk and I couldn't see a thing. Didn't even know I was driving on the sidewalk. It doesn't matter whether I was driving on the sidewalk or not. And it doesn't matter whether I was drunk or not drunk. I am not drunk. I only had a couple of drinks. *(Sits.)* In a court of law, if you're parked on the wrong direction, you don't have a leg to stand on. I don't know how much damage I did to your car, but I'm not paying for it. In fact, I think my car is embedded in yours. I may have totaled my car, and yours, too. What time is it?

JACK is dumbfounded. PAULA continues talking as she goes downstairs.

PAULA: I'm going down to see what the damage is, but I'm not paying for it because you were parked in the wrong direction, and that's illegal.

JACK: What did you say?

PAULA: I said you were parked in the wrong direction, and that that's illegal. That the front of the car doesn't reflect an oncoming car, so if you're coming into it, you can't see it. That it was too dark, and I didn't see it. That I couldn't even see the road. That my car is embedded in yours.

PAULA goes downstairs. JACK drops to the floor. PAULA's footsteps are heard. The upstage door opens. The lights of dawn are seen outside. JACK stands. He goes to the kitchen, reenters, looks around. He is dumbfounded.

JACK: *(Almost speechless.)* … Tressa …

TRESSA: *(Somnolent.)* … Yes … ?

JACK: Did you hear that?

TRESSA: … What … ?

JACK: Paula wrecked my car.

There is a silence. TRESSA snores.

JACK: *(To himself.)* … My car …

He prepares himself a cup of tea and walks up the ramp. He drinks. PAULA's footsteps are heard. She comes up the steps and sees him.

PAULA: It's okay. I think I dozed off for a moment there when I parked. I guess I must've dreamt I crashed. *(She goes to the landing, looks at JACK, and laughs.)* You look kind of scared. *(She goes to the table and sits.)* Is that tea you're drinking?

JACK looks at the cup, then looks at PAULA and speaks in a high-pitched voice.

JACK: Yes.

PAULA: May I have some?

JACK: Yes.

PAULA: *(Ingratiatingly.)* I'm glad I didn't wreck your car.

Pause.

JACK: *(In a squeaky high voice.)* Oh …

PAULA: Relieved?

JACK: Oh …

PAULA: Oh what?

JACK exits dumbfounded. TRESSA appears left. She is putting on a housecoat.

TRESSA: Hi.

PAULA: Hi.

TRESSA: What happened?

PAULA: Nothing.

TRESSA: You just got in?

PAULA: Just now.

TRESSA: How was the party?

PAULA: You're lucky you didn't come.

TRESSA: What?—Was it boring?

PAULA: Yes. It was depressing.

TRESSA: What happened?

PAULA: Nothing happened.—Dan and Flo were there.

TRESSA and JACK: Oh.

TRESSA stretches her neck.

PAULA: You're tired.

TRESSA: I'm going to bed. *(Starts to exit left.)*

PAULA: Yes, it's late.

TRESSA: Goodnight.

PAULA: Goodnight.

JACK: Goodnight. *(Reaches for his jacket and puts it on.)*

PAULA: Where are you going?

JACK: Going for a walk.

PAULA: Now?!

JACK: Yeah, I feel restless.

PAULA: Where're you going?

JACK: Out.

JACK kisses PAULA and starts to exit. PAULA is anxious.

PAULA: Be careful.

JACK: I will.

PAULA: *(Her anxiety builds.)* I'll go with you.

JACK: No, Paula.

PAULA: Please.

JACK: I want to be alone.

PAULA: *(Going on her knees by the railing)*: Where are you going? *(She waits a moment.)* Why, Jack? I'm worried! Let me go with you!

JACK: I'll be all right.

PAULA: Please! Jack! *(Silence.)* Jaaack!! Where are you going!!! Where are you going!!!

TRESSA enters from the kitchen. She and PAULA look at each other. PAULA stands.

PAULA: He went …

They embrace.

PAULA: Into the night. *(Sobs.)* Into the night … Into the night …

The lights fade.

It's 5:00 a.m. JACK is standing on the railing. His hands are tied behind him to the post. He is bare-chested. There is blood smeared on his chest. TRESSA stands left, PAULA right. They both face him.

JACK:
They wanted to fuck me and they
did. They fucked me till I was

blue in the face. One first and
then another and another. And
they came back. They couldn't
get enough. And I wanted all
they had. They didn't use
condoms. Nothing.

On the raw. I told them I was HIV-
positive.

They didn't care.

I did, and I handed them condoms.

And they didn't take them. They said
they had more pleasure without them.
I was bleeding like a faucet, and they
fucked me and fucked me, and it hurt
like the devil, and I screamed and
screamed till I couldn't scream anymore.
And they kept fucking me, one
after the other, and I never had so
much pleasure in my life.

I handed them condoms, and they
didn't care. I've never been so
happy in my life. One big cock
after the other. I screamed like a
goat in the slaughterhouse. I don't
know. I don't know. Did I think?
Did I think? I didn't think. I didn't
think when I got it. I just got it.
It's a virus. It happened when I got
fucked by someone. When you get
a cold, do you wonder who gave
it to you? No one gave it to me. I
got it. Maybe I got it when I got
the best fuck in my life. And then
maybe I got it into me when I got
a lousy fuck ... So what.

He puts his head down and sobs.

Don't touch me.

TRESSA:	PAULA:
Didn't they?	Didn't they, Jack?
You're not!	Why do you think you are?
Why did you say that?	Why, Jack?
Why did you say that?	Oh, Jack!
Did they know what a condom is?	
	Oh, Jack!
Did you think you were giving them AIDS?	
Oh ...	
Oh ...	
You don't have AIDS.	

Don't touch me.

I'm contagious.

I don't want to give you AIDS.

Sobs.

I have AIDS.

I'm contagious.

I have AIDS.
I have AIDS.
I have AIDS.
Yes. I am!

Why does he say
he has AIDS?

Jack, you don't
have AIDS.

Why does he say
that? Stop it,
Jack! Stop it.

You don't have AIDS.
And if you did, you
would never do what you
say you did. Jack, you would
never do that. Jack, you
have to protect yourself.
You don't have AIDS.
you're not HIV positive.
You have to be careful.
No. Remember.

What should I remember?

TRESSA: That you don't have AIDS. That you have been tested. Why do you think you have AIDS?

JACK is near fainting.

TRESSA: You don't have AIDS. You don't. You don't. I have seen your tests. You're not. You're not.

TRESSA reaches out to JACK as he descends. She holds him up as they walk back to the bench.

JACK: Because ... Because ... Because ...

She sits holding him on her lap in a Pietá position. She slides her hand on his chest.

TRESSA: All my life I've had a passion in me, and it is for you. All my life it was there, has been there, reserved for you. I never felt it. I never knew what passion was in me.—It was there, but only for you. I say "you" because I don't know what else to call you. I could call you Key, or Burst, or Debris, or Flood. You touched it, and it rose and burst out like a dike that opens to the force of the waters inside, and everything comes out—water, stones, boulders, trees. Like prisoners in a jail who think of nothing but escape day and night, year after year, and when the riot breaks out and the doors crack and burst open because of the force of the explosion, as if it were of dynamite, or the eruption of a volcano underneath the floors, when the force of the prisoners' desire for freedom erupts, and the walls burst, and the stones and the water rush through the opening ferociously, wildly, and fearlessly. It is like that. It feels like that. You touched it, and it rose and burst out—water, hard stones, branches, gravel, mud, foam ... out of my chest ... for you ... Burst. Let me call you Burst.

PAULA kneels next to them. Her head is on JACK's knees. A blazing fire is projected on them. A gust of wind blows on them while JACK starts lifting his head slowly. TRESSA and PAULA start looking up. The voice of the High Lama and the music of the film are heard as they speak. Stormy Wagnerian music joins in.

The HIGH LAMA's VOICE and PAULA: "I have waited for you, my child, for a long time. I believe you will live through the storm. And after, through the long age of desolation, you may still live, growing older and wiser and more patient."

TRESSA joins their voices.

The HIGH LAMA's VOICE, PAULA, and TRESSA: "You will conserve the fragrance of our history and add to it the touch of your own mind. You will welcome the stranger,"

JACK joins their voices.

The HIGH LAMA's VOICE, PAULA, TRESSA, and JACK: "and teach him the rule of age and wisdom, and one of these strangers, it may be, will succeed you when you are yourself very old. Beyond that, my vision weakens, but I see, at a great distance, a new world stirring in the ruins, stirring clumsily but in hopefulness, seeking its lost and legendary treasure. And they will all be here, my children, hidden behind the mountains in the valley of Shangri-la, preserved as by a miracle for a new Renaissance ... "

The volume of the music increases as the lights fade to black.

It is 8:00 a.m. TRESSA is standing on the steps. She wears a bathrobe. PAULA stands by the table. She is finishing putting her clothes in a suitcase on the table. She wears a light coat.

TRESSA: He's still asleep. Should I wake him?

PAULA puts the last garments in the suitcase.

PAULA: Let him sleep.

TRESSA goes to the bench.

PAULA: I'll wait a while. I want to see him before I go. *(Closes the suitcase.)* He's going through the worst time. *(Sits at the table.)* I'd like to ask him to come up and spend a few days with us.

TRESSA lies on the downstage bench.

TRESSA: That would be good for him. That would be good. To spend a few days in the country.

PAULA: Yes it would ... to spend a few days in the open. He likes it there. *(Goes to armchair and sits.)* Maybe when the play closes ... a week or two.

TRESSA: Yes. *(Pulls covers over her.)* That would be good for him. He's going through a very hard time ...

PAULA: Yes ... You go to sleep, Tressa. You must be tired. I'll wait for him.

TRESSA: *(As she turns and closes her eyes.)* ... Yes, Paula ... I'm tired.

The lights fade slightly as JACK enters from the bedroom. He is wrapped in a blanket, walks slowly to the upstage bench and sits. PAULA and TRESSA slowly turn towards him.

JACK: ... I'm tired ... I can't go back to sleep ...

His head and torso curve slightly toward the pillow. The lights fade slowly as JACK lets out a soft cry. The lights go to black.

About the Author

★ ★ ★ ★ ★ ★ ★ ★ ★

Maria Irene Fornes is widely admired as a playwright, director, and teacher of playwriting. A nine-time Obie Award-winner, she has written over forty plays, musicals, adaptations, and bi-lingual works, including *Fefu and Her Friends*, *Mud*, *Abingdon Square*, *Life is a Dream*, *The Summer in Gossensass*, *Promenade*, and *Letters from Cuba*. For more than four decades, Fornes has been associated with many important theatres producing new work, such as the Judson Poets' Theatre, The Actor's Workshop of San Francisco, American Place Theatre, Padua Hills Playwrights' Workshop and Festival, Theatre for the New City, La MaMa, Caffe Cino, and The Women's Project. In the 1970s she helped to found the playwright-producing organization known as New York Theatre Strategy, and at the same time she began her long association with INTAR, Hispanic American Arts Center, in New York City, directing the influential Hispanic Playwrights Lab that has had a profound effect on the development of American writers for the stage. Maria Irene Fornes has been honored as a member of the American Academy and Institute of Arts and Letters. She has also received the NEA Distinguished Artist Fellowship for Lifetime Achievement in Theatre and the PEN/Laura Pels Foundation Award for Drama as a Master American dramatist. She was born in Havana, Cuba and came to the U.S. in 1945.